THE
NULLARBOR
KID

THE NULLARBOR KID

Stories from my trucking life

RAY GILLELAND

ALLEN&UNWIN

SYDNEY · MELBOURNE · AUCKLAND · LONDON

First published in 2012

Allen & Unwin
Sydney, Melbourne, Auckland, London

83 Alexander Street
Crows Nest NSW 2065
Australia
Phone: (61 2) 8425 0100
Email: info@allenandunwin.com
Web: www.allenandunwin.com

Cataloguing-in-Publication details are available
from the National Library of Australia
www.trove.nla.gov.au

ISBN 978 1 74237 949 4

Set in 13/18 pt Bembo by Midland Typesetters, Australia
Printed and bound in Australia by Griffin Press

10 9 8 7 6 5 4 3 2 1

Contents

Prologue

There are not many of us left now. The years have taken their toll on those who were there at the beginning of long-distance road transport in Australia. I am talking of the Golden Age of transport, the 1950s. This book is about the trucks and drivers of that far-off time.

The roads are so much better now, and the trucks are more powerful. Driver comfort has improved out of sight. Padded interiors, sleeping bunks, television sets, microwave ovens, mobile telephones, navigation aids. To us old-timers who did it the hard way, it's like a fairytale come true. Freeways and all-sealed roads have emerged from the single ribbons of bitumen and gravel tracks that we had to use.

Now, there is no hill so steep that it can sap the strength of a truck so that you wonder if you'll make it. But there were quite a few in our day. One Tree Hill comes to mind, south of Gunning. Many a time I had to zigzag up that hill, back and forth from one side to the other, in low gear, nearly to the point of stalling, hoping no one would come shooting over the top towards me while I was on their side of the narrow piece of bitumen. There were some that didn't make it and had to get a tow to the top after reversing into the side of the bank. Imagine the terror gripping the driver as he willed his truck not to stop on the wrong side of the road in the darkness of night, and then, if it did stall, trying to get 20 or 30 tons slipping backwards on fourteen wheels off the road safely, with only a couple of brake jabs possible before there was no air left. It was all part of the job back then—no ifs or buts, just get the load to its destination somehow, anyhow. And, you know, we did.

The trucks were all underpowered for the loads they carried—usually six cylinders and a five-speed gearbox, some with a transfer box to help. A basic thin seat squeezed between the door and the metal-covered motor, a hand-signal arm attached to the door, a weakly powered windscreen wiper hanging from the top of the windscreen that the wind blew up over the roof just when it was needed most, and a small rear-view mirror attached to the top of the cabin that was as big as a lady's compact mirror. In some trucks the driver's seat wasn't even in line with the steering wheel and pedals. It was as if they'd designed the truck and at the last minute thought, *Oh, it needs a driver—shove a seat in there somewhere.*

I am eighty years old; time dims the memory, and many are gone who would have helped in making this book a clearer window on history. Names have been forgotten over time, and so many tales of those days remain untold. But I hope you enjoy the stories and photographs that are here. I ask but one thing. When you have closed the book, pause for a second and, with a smile and a nod, give them their due. They were drivers.

1
Cinderella on wheels

Why are the Australian long-distance transport industry Cinderella and the state governments the Ugly Sisters? How did things evolve from yesteryear to today? Let's look at how it all started, way back in the seventeenth century.

The Dutch East India Company had an established outpost in the East Indies and a lucrative trade in spices sold in Europe. The Dutch explorer Abel Tasman had a peek at Tasmania while looking for more spice islands, but good old Abe couldn't smell any spice so gave it a miss.

Then in 1770 Captain James Cook grabbed a large hunk of land further north, over the horizon from the non-spice isle. He barged into it after leaving New Zealand, not realising how big it was. He was on his way to the Cape of Good

Hope and home. Planting the Union Jack at Botany Bay, he claimed the land only to a longitude from around Darwin to South Australia.

When Jimmy C arrived home in London the Poms were happy that he had plonked their flag on an elusive bit of land down in the South Seas. They had been looking for the mythical Great South Land for years. It was thought there was a large land mass down there to balance the large land mass in the northern hemisphere. They didn't know if this was the Great South Land, but any large chunk of land down there was a plus.

Now what to do with it? They had no idea. 'Best thing: file it away in a drawer. Something will pop up one day and we'll dig it out and find a use for it.'

At this time underfed kids were pinching silver buckles from the shoes of the gentry and doing other such thieving to buy food. Even some of the grown-ups were poaching M'Lord's pheasants and rabbits. Some of the Irish were demanding self-rule—the upstarts. There were hard times in England at the end of the eighteenth century for the masses of ordinary folk.

'Really, these people must learn to put up with things and keep their place in society' was the government's general feeling. Well, the general feeling of all those who were doing okay, that is. 'What to do? The prisons are full. The Royal Navy's ships aren't needed, because we're not fighting the French (not at the moment, anyway), and those ships are being used as prisons, but they are nearly full as well.

It's getting too much. These people must stop breaking the law.'

Then it was remembered. 'Ah yes! Lost in the files. That damned place Cook found years ago down in the South Seas somewhere. It's doing nothing but supply a home for strange animals and dark people. Let's make some use of it. Ship all the nuisances down there—good riddance!—and see what happens. We'll send that Arthur Phillip fellow with a few leaky ships. They might get there . . . Anyway, that's it. Done.'

The leaky ships did arrive, in 1788, and settled at Sydney, eighteen years after Jimmy C had planted the flag at Botany Bay.

The First Fleet was a mixed bag: prisoners, free settlers and some 'black sheep' types needing to be out of sight of society. Only a few days after the fleet arrived at Sydney Cove, the French admiral La Perouse showed up, poking around the Pacific. Arthur P gave him some supplies and saw him off. That was a close one—we might all have ended up 'frogs' with the kangaroos and koalas.

'Well,' said the Poms a few years later, 'let's use up all of the land, seeing as we have people now in Sydney Town, Hobart and Brisbane. The French are poking around that land on the western coast again. We had better plonk some of our wretches over there. That way, we can claim the whole damned continent and forget about them.' And that's what they did. The little island of Tasmania had been running its own affairs for years. By 1839, Perth, Melbourne, Adelaide and Darwin were European settlements. All this happened in a period of fifty-one years. Each colony then did its own thing and went its own way.

On the mainland the British expanded into the interior from each toehold on this huge hunk of land. Bullock drays and, as time went on, railways snaked further inland to bring back grain and produce to the capital cities. The colonies had little to do with each other, preferring their own Pommy-type empire. A form of jealousy even existed: a 'We are better than them' attitude. This persists today, regardless of what anyone says to the contrary.

Anyway, in the nineteenth century it was decided that the colonies had better get their act together, as there was talk of the Russians coming. No, not the communists: long before them, Imperial Russia was thought to be eyeing off titbits of land around the world to be colonised. So the colonies built forts with huge cannons trained out to sea and waited. Nothing happened. The guns remained silent. (Some are still there.) But then it was thought by the five colonies on the mainland that it would be advantageous to combine as one country. Hooray! Oh, and Tassie as well, for what it's worth.

The dawn of the twentieth century saw the birth of the Commonwealth of Australia. And about time too.

Someone said, 'We may be joined in name, but we certainly aren't joined in any practical sense.'

'How do you mean?' asked someone else.

'Well, why did you use an Irish railway engineer to lay your rail system?'

'Well, why did *you* engage a Scot?'

'None of your business. We don't have to answer to you.'

'And neither do we to you . . . so there.'

The rail gauges were all different sizes—they didn't match. What folly! It was more like Europe's many different countries than five branches of the same family that had started as Pommy colonies.

Perth was stuck way down in the south-west corner. In fact, Perth is the most isolated capital city in the world today. Adelaide wasn't that important—not a large population. The two antagonists with the most to gain or lose were New South Wales and Victoria.

Remember, dear reader, that this was in the early 1900s. Trains on land and steamers around the coast were the only ways to move people and freight interstate. Ships were slow, and the various state governments owned the railways: they were not private enterprises. Goods were delivered around the cities and towns by horses and drays. There were water troughs on street corners for the horses. These were later replaced by garages with rows of petrol pumps out the front for the mechanical horses on wheels that were emerging.

Now, do you see where I'm taking you? The twentieth century saw the arrival and continual improvement of electricity, radio, telephone, aircraft, and, wait for it . . . the *motor vehicle*.

The Second World War escalated improvement in many areas, including the motor lorry. Trucks then were larger than today's semitrailers; they could carry huge and heavy loads across longer distances. They were slow, but they could do it. But the rail system in Australia remained the same—nothing had changed. To send goods interstate by rail involved trucking the goods to the railhead, taking them by that state's rail system to the border, transhipping them onto a different rail system to the city of destination, and finally trucking them again, from the rail yard to the customer. How quick! How very modern! (How the hell couldn't they see that times had moved on?)

Industry was looking for more efficient methods of handling goods. Time and damage were problems with the rail system. Ex-servicemen returned from the war had money and were looking for opportunities. There was one staring them in the face, lit up like a neon sign. It seemed to be shouting, 'Look at me!' and they did. The penny dropped. A better way would be to load the consignment onto a truck at origin and deliver it direct to the customer. It would be far more efficient and much quicker. *Buy a truck and away we go*, they thought. That's when long-distance road transport really got its start.

Mind you, there were no superhighways back then, just narrow bitumen roads that followed the original Cobb & Co. stagecoach routes that joined country towns. By grinding from town to town, up and down mountains, over one-lane wooden bridges and many long gravel sections, always prepared to stop in a hurry to allow sheep and cattle to have right of way, the truck driver would finally reach his destination, 500, 700, 1000 miles away, even 3000 miles away. All this was accomplished with vehicles made in another country based on models that belonged to the 1930s. They were able to carry heavy loads not very fast, and their braking systems were so inefficient that they were notoriously dangerous. These trucks, the only ones available, were not suited for this hunk of land with blistering heat, steep mountains and vast distances.

The state governments viewed this upstart industry as a threat to their rail system, and, yes, it was. The new breed was determined not to be kept chained to the old ways and to the thinking of governments that were blinkered in their attitude to progress. Then there was the establishment's fury at those interfering with the status quo. They had to be stopped.

The state government railways had an iron-clad monopoly on the transportation of all goods further than 50 miles. Trucks carrying goods were taxed after that distance. 'You truck fellers,' they were told, 'can run around in the cities and towns and bring the goods to the rail for us. The horse and dray are getting a little slow these days. But don't get any bright ideas to try to compete with us: it's not allowed. We won't let you.' Half of the road tax was given to the state railways each year to help with the losses they managed to accumulate through their inefficient rail system and monopoly-type thinking.

Then the state governments imposed a tax for goods carried by road in competition with their railways. The charge was 3 pence for every ton, including the weight of the truck, multiplied by each mile of the journey. A truck had to be fully loaded all the time. It made for an enormous amount of money for each trip. Weighbridges were few and far between and kept shop hours. Drivers had to load in a hit-and-miss style, watching the truck springs and hoping they were about legal. Tolerance of axle weights in each state varied, and this added to the hardship.

If it had been only the freight that was taxed it would probably have been workable. Taxing the weight of the truck on each trip penalised the truck owner. It was cash up front: pay before you go. The permit was dated with allowance times for the trip in question, and if a breakdown put the date out there was the risk of a fine as well, unless it could be proved without a shadow of a doubt it was genuine. As usual, drivers were guilty till proved innocent.

Road transport inspectors were given wide powers to intercept trucks anywhere and at any time, day or night, to check permits and if necessary weigh the truck on the nearest railway yard weighbridge. The inspectors were issued with keys to unlock the railway yard gates at night. A driver could drive for twenty-four hours straight if he could or wanted to—no one cared. Inspectors were only interested in the weight, and in what goods were on the truck, as some goods like refrigerators had a cheaper tax. (The railways didn't want them: too much damage.) They also looked for mixed loads, in case the correct tax hadn't been paid.

The intent was obvious: if this interstate road transport industry could not be stopped then it would be milked for all its worth. The challenge was enormous. And so began the Great Game: private interstate transport versus state government railways.

Victoria banned all commercial vehicles from its roads

An Albion HD on an east–west trip with a double-deck of crated refrigerators. (Courtesy Jim Boler.)

between midnight Saturday and midnight Sunday. New South Wales decided to ban all trucks from the highways within 50 miles of Sydney between 10 am and 4 pm on Sunday. All hotels were shut in New South Wales on Sunday, but if you were a bona fide traveller—that is, you'd travelled more than 45 miles on a Sunday—then you could with your drivers licence demand a drink at a hotel. (This meant the thirsty public could gallop out to a hotel over 45 miles away, get sloshed, then wander home again. No booze bus in those days.) The watering holes closest to the city on the three main roads in to Sydney but still outside the 50-mile zone were at Gosford on the north road, Narellan on the south and Penrith on the west. It was difficult to find parking space for a truck on the way in to Sydney during curfew hours, and what better place to wait after you'd driven your 45 miles than a hotel, and then all go home together?

I wish I could show you the pictures stored in my head of the things we did and got away with, and the things we did and didn't get away with. If only you could have met that determined breed of Aussie with the attitude that there was no problem that could not be overcome—there were many of them. They were rough and tough but could laugh at trouble and at themselves. What an adventurous time it was back then.

But the battle still goes on today. The players are the same but the stakes are higher. There are so many nitpicking regulations it's beyond a joke. For example, if a driver today misspells in his log book the town name where he takes his rest period he loses points and has to pay a fine, sometimes in the thousands. And there are not enough rest stops to fit the regulations. Also, it is against the law to park in towns late at night; drivers must be parked in designated areas that are not, however, yet built. It seems the Ugly Sisters are still giving Cinderella a hard time and will continue to do so at every chance they get. Where the bloody hell is Prince Charming?

2

Looking for a dream

What a magical year: 1931. Different from any other year. 'Why?' you ask. Because on 28 October 1931 I was born. I was a mistake, but what a glorious mistake! I grew up during the Depression and the Second World War in Ramsgate on the edge of Botany Bay. I could look across the bay to where Captain Cook landed in 1770.

It was a tough time, a changing time. Australia was part of the British Empire and proud of it. They said that 'the sun never sets on the British Empire,' meaning of course that it was so large and scattered that there was always daylight shining on it somewhere. Empire Night was cracker night, with bonfires in yards and paddocks and us kids lighting and throwing the largest 'bungers' you could imagine at each other. Sky Rockets, Jumping Jacks: we saved for ages to buy those now-banned, dangerous horrors. We got the odd burn or two, but that's all; we didn't think they were dangerous.

Dad had many cars. There was a Fiat, a Hupmobile, a Chandler, an Oakland and a 1935 Ford sedan that he kept from 1939 to 1949.

When war was declared in 1939 it didn't seem real to us little boys at school. We sang 'There'll Always Be an England' and all that patriotic stuff at assembly, but it was all too far away. Dad was in a protected industry.

Then all of a sudden it was a new ball game: Japan was our enemy, and Japan was very close—just up there a little bit on the map. Events started to move fast. All the street signs, railway stations signs—anything that could help the enemy— were taken down. Brown paper strips were glued all over the glass in windows to stop it shattering from a bomb blast in an air raid. During the day the sky was always full of planes— fighters, bombers, trainers—we lived near the main Sydney airport. Air-raid sirens were hooked up all over the city and were practised every day at midday to test that they were working. It was the 'all clear' signal they used, a continual note, not the air-raid warning signal, which wailed up and down.

Petrol rationing came into force. Some cars were fitted with charcoal burners on the back bumper bar so that once the motor had been started with petrol and had heated up, petrol could be substituted with gas from the burner. A few people had huge gas bags fitted to the roof of their car on a metal frame. (The war ended in 1945, but we had petrol rationing for the next four years, till 1949.) All cars and trucks were only allowed enough petrol each month to cover a few miles. Headlights had to be fitted with a slotted metal cover with the louvres projecting the light onto the road but cutting out any glare up into the night sky. As most cars were a dark colour, a white strip had to be painted around the lower edge of the car body to help avoid collisions in the blackout.

At school an air-raid drill was carried out once every week during class time. There was never an actual real-life air raid, but we had plenty of practice. Our playground was dug up to make slit trenches that zigzagged. When we asked why they didn't just make long trenches we were told it was so that if we were machine-gunned from the air they couldn't get us all at once. Sounded sensible.

My seat in class was next to the door. Beside the door was a wooden first-aid box as big as a suitcase, painted white with a red cross on the top. I'm sure there were enough metal implements and wooden things and ointments and bandages to come to the aid of the whole British Army. The box had a handle on the top of the lid, and an adult would have been able to carry it easily. I was a skinny eleven-year-old kid who happened to sit next to the box—that's all—but it was my responsibility to get the box to the trenches when the air-raid warning was sounded. Everybody else overtook me swiftly while I was huffing and puffing along, trying to swap it from hand to hand as it became heavier. I always arrived last after starting out first. But the first-aid kit had to get to the trenches

17

as early as possible, and my teacher could not leave till the last boy was out and running. I suggested that as I was only the third-fastest runner perhaps the first-aid box should be given to one of the faster runners.

It was pointed out that they were in a different class.

I offered to swap classes.

The offer was refused.

I suggested the teacher carry it.

That was dismissed with the comment 'Shut up, Gilleland. Just run faster.'

I was stuck with it.

To top it off, the ground beneath our playground was all clay. After rain the trench system filled with water and was actually a zigzagging muddy yellow canal system. In a real air raid we would have been bombed or drowned, depending on where we happened to be at the time.

Then the war came to our shores. It was 1942, and the Japanese had bombed Darwin and Townsville. One night late in May the air-raid sirens went off. Dad and Mum moved the dining room table into the hall and we all hid underneath it as Sydney Harbour exploded with the noise of depth charges seeking Japanese midget submarines that had penetrated the boom gates at the harbour entrance and were torpedoing ships. At the same time a large submarine shelled the eastern suburbs. We had no idea what it was all about, but we certainly could hear all the explosions and the continuous wail of the sirens.

The war was over. I was ready to leave school, and Dad asked me what I wanted to do with my life.

'I want to drive.'

'Drive what?'

'Anything.'

'Do you want to be a mechanic?'

'Don't think so . . . just drive, you know, just chase the horizon.'

'Okay, you don't know what you want to do yet, so I'll teach you to be a cutter in the garment trade.'

I learnt it in just over a year and became the youngest cutter for Country Club shirts, the premier shirt on the market at the time. I also bought my first car: a 1927 'baby' Austin. I was always looking for a driving job. Each night after coming home from work on the train I would repair my baby so I could go for a spin on the weekend. She was a typical baby, always misbehaving when you wanted to show her off.

A mate from school had his own truck: a Bedford. He was only seventeen, and was I envious of him and his wealthy family. I decided that the only way to catch him up was to go out into the bush and work for big money.

So I packed my bags, and Mum and Dad wished me luck. I was off, looking for my dream. It was out there somewhere—I just had to find it. The kid from Botany Bay was on his way.

3

No Tree Plain

The Latin words *null* and *arbor* translate to 'no tree'. The Nullarbor Plain, or No Tree Plain, is the vast desert area of thousands of square miles on the central south coast of Australia west of Adelaide. The plain actually is almost treeless, although there are bushes and shrubs. If it rains, colourful wildflowers come out, but mostly it's just dry desert, hot and dusty by day and freezing cold at night. The plain is the home of rabbits, wombats, dingoes, cattle, sheep, turkeys, scorpions, snakes and camels. Being on the Nullarbor Plain is like being at the beginning of the world. It is all so vast, so primitive, and just a bit scary. After a few days out there you feel you're the only one left on earth. I used to talk aloud to my truck, just to hear my voice. 'Hot today, old girl,' or 'Okay, time for a stop. You're doing very well,' or, at other times, very loudly and angrily, 'Not another puncture?'

The Nullarbor Plain, 1955.

The Nullarbor Plain today—they call it 'across the paddock.'

In the 1950s, the road across the plain, which was just a rough dirt and sand track but 1000 miles long, was part of the only route connecting the civilised east coast with Perth. We early pioneer drivers, who numbered fewer than the fingers on both hands, transported goods along it from one side of Australia to the other—3000 miles all-up of the driest, hottest, toughest, deadliest country that a truck driver would ever be asked to cross. It was a new chapter in the new industry of long-distance road transport.

From Sydney through the eastern states of New South Wales, Victoria and part of South Australia there was a narrow sealed road with some sections of gravel. Then, after leaving Port Augusta, at the top of the Spencer Gulf in South Australia, it was that long dirt track across the uninhabited desert till the little town of Norseman in Western Australia was reached. The last 500-odd miles into Perth also had a few gravel stretches. It was quite a trek.

Once a driver set off with a load no one knew where he was till he arrived at his next destination, two days, five days, even weeks later. There were a few scattered properties off the main track that only knew we were around if we took mail in to them. That was a bonus, actually, as they would use their primitive wirelesses to notify those further on that we were coming. If we had no mail then no one knew we were out there, so any emergency affecting us had to be fixed by us.

The landowners on the Nullarbor Plain had properties that were measured in thousands of square miles, not acres. The winding sandy track passed through some of the properties many miles away from the homesteads, and the occasional fence had a gate that we had to stop and open, drive through, stop and shut again. A six-month jail sentence if you were caught leaving one open.

A gate marking a property boundary, Nullarbor Plain.

Some drivers were paid trip money, an amount for each trip they finished, including expenses. Others were paid a weekly wage plus an amount on each trip for expenses.

The equipment we drove was basic: plain, slow and reliable. No flashy paint or chrome! Truck and trailer, usually fourteen wheels, crash gearbox, brass worm drive differentials, basic six-cylinder diesel motors, metal and wooden cabins that shook so badly that the doors would sometimes fall off onto the road.

The only extras were fog lights and spotlights fitted to the heavy front bumper bar. But problems could still flare up, like broken springs needing to be wired together till a place could be found to park and fit a new leaf, or a broken centre bolt or a wheel bearing that had given up the ghost. All these extras were carried in an extensive toolbox underneath the trailer, as there was nothing out there but you and your ability to get out of trouble.

The 1954 AEC Matador was a good, reliable truck, as was the Albion HD model. They were both fitted with a straight six-cylinder engine and a five-speed gearbox. The British trucks—Leyland, AEC, Albion, Thornycroft, Foden, Atkinson —formed the backbone of Australia's transport in those days, as they attracted minimal sales tax compared to European and American trucks. The British trucks were available immediately from the dealer's floor. Anything else had to be ordered from overseas and took up to nine months for delivery. You would see the odd Mack, Federal, Diamond T and Mercedes-Benz on the road, but not in great numbers. International 180s and Ford 500s also started to appear. The trailers were single or dual axles, McGrath or Freighter, and the Fruehauf was arriving on the market.

Enough fuel and water had to be carried from one side of the country to the other. There were a few water tanks scattered across the desert but they were usually dry, so it was in your best interest to be self-sufficient as much as possible. I had a 44-gallon drum of water, and I also carried around 200 gallons of diesel on each trip.

Water tanks under a corrugated-iron roof erected to catch rain.

Only a few fresh food lines were taken, as nothing fresh lasted longer than a couple of days out there in the heat and dust, and they were bought at the last outpost. There was no air-conditioning or portable refrigerators back then. The main foods were fruit in season, like apples, oranges and so on, and tinned food—tomato soup, baked beans, Irish stew, peaches, pears—anything in a tin. I had a primus stove, and I always carried a second tin-opener, just in case. I bet you have never tried to open a tin of baked beans with a hammer and chisel. It can be messy, believe me, and worse—the sauce spurts up into your face or the can tilts over into the dust and half the beans are lost on the ground.

Any repairs had to be handled by the driver. No mechanics, service stations or tyre repair shops out there. You went across the desert at your own peril. Get into trouble? Get out of it yourself or don't go. Sometimes a driver might send a telegram advising of a breakdown or some problem, but he almost never made a telephone call, as there were not many phones and it was expensive. It wasn't the trucks that made history; it was the drivers. We made antiquated equipment produced in another country do things it was not designed to do.

4
Memory lane

I tilted my stetson a bit further over my eyes. The desert gave off a hazy, white-hot glare that made you squint; it had that whitish, pale-blue sky above that seemed to ripple with the heat. In the 1950s few people braved the dirt track across the Nullarbor Plain, particularly in January—the middle of summer. But it was the only way across Australia from the east coast to the west.

My green 30-ton Albion HD semitrailer wasn't in my good books. Another unwanted stop hundreds of miles from anywhere. I called her the Perth Express—what a laugh. Her top speed was 38 miles per hour, going downhill with a tailwind, but out here on such a rough track in no-man's land I was lucky to coax her along at 20 miles per hour.

The Perth Express, Albion HD model. The windscreen opened out, and there were small air vents in front of the cab. She also featured spotlights, fog lights and an illegal air horn on top of the cab.

I knew what was wrong with her, and it was becoming annoying. This was the third time in two days the old girl had split her copper fuel line somewhere, cracked from the vibrations, finally sucking in more air than fuel and shuddering to a stop. And I wasn't happy. No sir. It was easy to get angry out here.

The fuel line had to be repaired. To hunt down a small crack in a copper pipe that stretched from the two fuel tanks along the chassis, under the cab and up to the motor was no fun. Once it was found, I would have to cut it out, flare the two ends and join them tightly with a connector, maybe even cut out a length and install a new piece. Then I had to bleed the system to remove every bit of air by hand-pumping the fuel back up to the inline pump. I would loosen the fuel line at the injectors, then remove the side cover on the inline pump, insert a screwdriver at the base of each spring-encircled valve and prise the valve up and down, pumping the fuel up to each injector. Cover back on pump, clamp injector lines shut. It usually took only a couple of turns of the starter for the motor to fire and quickly rid the system of any odd bubbles of air, and then, hey presto, I'd be on my way again.

I opened the toolbox lid and, as usual, bits and pieces fell out onto the ground. Ignoring them, I pulled out a piece of tarpaulin about the size of a tablecloth and with an angry grunt threw it under the trailer along with a small bag of tools. I flattened the tarp out and put the tool bag on it as a pillow, unbuckled my gun belt, hung my hat on the spare-wheel rack next to me and flopped down onto the ground. I was hot, sweaty and cranky, in no mood to start crawling around under the chassis in this heat trying to locate the split.

Before I ventured underneath I carefully surveyed all around, checking to see there were no snakes or scorpions in the dust to bite me on the bum or wherever might take their fancy. An extremely careful look around, I can assure you. The death adder is not very large and isn't an aggressive snake, but it is extremely well camouflaged and will lie motion-less till you nearly step on it, and then strike like lightning. A bite from one and I'd be dead before anybody wandering across the desert found me. I carried a .45 Colt pistol and a Winchester .25-20 rifle, and wore Leatherneck boots made by RM Williams. They were like a sixteenth-century pirate's boots that came up nearly to the knees and had a folded top. If you had come across me out there you would have seen a tall, slim young man, brown from the sun, wearing a battered old stetson and a pair of swimming trunks, with a pistol hanging from his waist, walking around in pirate's boots. What a sight!

Okay, no snakes or scorpions. A quick swig from the water bag, then I crawled underneath.

•

I lay on the tarpaulin looking back out the way I had come, under the trailer axle, hoping to see a car or truck and knowing all the time that it was not going to happen: I hadn't seen anybody for days. My mind started to wander through those days gone by, when I was a youngster. All I'd wanted to do was chase the horizon and see what I couldn't yet see. *Well, look around you, stupid*, was my next thought. *Happy? Is this what you wanted to see?*

Shut up, I answered myself. *I'll get myself out of this one; I'm just having a little rest.*

I looked out to my left towards the desert, which disappeared into the heat haze, and I started to trace my life's journey to this isolated spot in this primitive land. I conjured up a slide show of pictures in my mind.

I was a kid again; it was the 1930s. I could see it all as

if it were yesterday. The postman delivered mail by walking from house to house twice a day, morning and afternoon, and once on Saturday morning, carrying all the letters in a huge leather bag over his shoulder. If a household had mail they knew it, because he blew a whistle as he slipped the letter into the postbox. The telegram boy had a pushbike to deliver his telegrams, as they were expensive and urgent.

There were no supermarkets in those days—all our food was from the small local shops every few miles along the bus routes or tramlines throughout the suburbs. The milkman, baker and iceman all delivered to the door of each house every day by horse and cart. How we looked out for that iceman. There were always slivers of ice handed out to be sucked. Then the clothes prop man came round every week or so. Freshly washed clothes were hung on two washing lines stretched across the backyard, usually every Monday. It needed at least two long tree branches with a fork on the end to keep the lines from drooping and dangling the clean clothes on the ground. The weight of the clothes on the lines was so heavy that a clothes prop didn't last very long, so the clothes prop man's call of 'Clothes props!' down the street was always welcome. The man selling rabbits had a loud voice too, for his familiar call of 'Rabbito, rabbito, two and six a pair.' It was a frequent sound in the quiet streets.

●

My mouth was dry; I decided I needed another drink. I crawled out on all fours from under the trailer, reminding myself to go easy on the water as I had a long way to travel and only the two water bags. I had a swig from the bag hanging on the tie rail, frowned at the bit of fuel line I could see along the chassis and decided to just lie under the trailer in the shade; I wasn't in the mood to tackle it yet.

•

Now, where was I? When I was about nine years old I would sit on the side of the road, in the gutter, and write down on a bit of paper all the numberplates of trucks as they went past. What did I do with them? Buggered if I know. But I loved those trucks. The look, the smell, the noise—there was nothing like it. They mesmerised me. One truck driver shook his fist at me. Why, I don't know, but we weren't into finger gestures back then so I screwed my face up and poked my tongue out at him.

Motor trucks started to be seen more often, a few with hard tyres then more and more with pump-up tyres. They had wooden cabins, no doors—just a rail at the edge of the seat like a stagecoach, to stop the driver slipping out sideways—and a canvas blind that could be rolled down if it rained. Then they started to get doors: half-doors at first, then full doors with glass windows!

I pestered Dad for my driving licence, and soon after the war I got it. I could drive anything but a bus, a taxi and a motorbike. I didn't want to drive a bus, a taxi or a motorbike; I wanted to drive a truck and go places, and that was what I intended to do. That bit of paper said I could.

First, though, a car: the little 1927 Austin 7. Then a standard two-door coupé, and then a 1936 Austin panel van that had no starter: I had to hand-crank it. That's when I learnt to hold a crank handle the correct way. Dad showed me. You don't hold the handle like a broom or a stick; you have the thumb on the same side as the fingers, like a scoop, so that if it backfires as you crank it, it will throw your hand away instead of breaking your thumb.

Okay, so the Austin panel van wasn't a big truck, but it was a start. My first proper truck was an old Ford, and then I had Blitz wagons, Inter K-5s and Austins and Bedfords after that, plus a Morris-Commercial. A printing mob I worked for had a 5-ton Commer and a small Hillman panel van. One wet day in Sydney I was going up George Street in the Hillman. Its wheel base was exactly the width of the tramlines. It had a worn gearbox and I was changing gear and stuck it into reverse by mistake. Luckily, the wheels skidded backwards on the wet tramlines and I quickly plucked it out and got the right gear, no damage done.

My first semitrailer was a Commer R7. Cover Girl was her name. That started my habit of naming all my trucks as the years went on. Didn't she get me into trouble ... She was the very first gooseneck low-loader type of car carrier in Australia.

•

I switched off the slide show in my head with a smile and came back to the present, as I crawled back out into the sun and stood up. 'Now, you,' I yelled as I kicked at the spare-wheel rack, 'what a laugh! The Perth Express? Always busting bloody fuel lines. We'll never get to Perth if you keep this up.'

Nothing changes much, I thought, as I stuck my stetson back on my head and ambled up to the front of the trailer, squinting once again into that bloody awful landscape. *Nothing changes much out here—it's always trouble.* But do you know what my next thought was? *I wouldn't change it for anything. Now, I need a 9/16 spanner and a piece of rag.*

5

Puncture problems

Drivers carried spare tyres for the prime mover and the trailer, but sooner or later, after the spares were used up, punctures had to be repaired. That was on every trip. The most popular jack for handling flat tyres was the bottle hydraulic type. We always carried a thick, hard, square piece of timber, sometimes two, to make a base for the jack on soft ground, of which there was hundreds of miles across the Nullarbor Plain.

Once the wood was settled firmly, the hydraulic jack was pumped a number of times to make a firm connection with the axle and also to test the ground—that it was hard enough to stand the weight without sinking sideways. As soon as firmness was reached but the weight was still on the wheel, the driver then 'broke' each wheel nut using the wheel spanner with a length of heavy metal pipe slipped over it to make the handle longer and give more purchase. The term 'break' was used to describe the cracking sound the nut made when first moved from its clamp position on the wheel. It was best to go all the way around the wheel, ascertaining that every nut would unwind without a problem and that there would not be a stubborn one at the end. It was usual to have ten wheel nuts to undo, or five, sometimes six, for a spyder wheel.

The driver had to be careful to see that each nut was returned to the exact stud from which it was removed. An easy way to do this was to lay the nuts out in a circle a little way away exactly as they were on the wheel. I also marked the twelve o'clock stud with a bit of spit on the hub. Then if the hub turned slightly I could still return the nuts to the correct stud. Why did we go to such lengths? Over the years, sometimes the threads could be cross-threaded on a nut, meaning that it tightened up okay but if it was accidentally put on another stud then the slightly different thread could cause a problem. The driver ended up with the nut and stud not being compatible and maybe after a lot of fiddling another cross-threaded nut. It was a bloody tiring business, continually trying to start these misfits, so the best thing was to make sure that as they came off, back they went on, each nut to its companion stud. Much easier.

With a ten-stud wheel, the nearest top stud was the last to be undone completely. This kept the wheel hanging on the studs rather than toppling on top of you. With all the nuts off, the driver would stand with his back to the wheel and reach out behind him, grasping the top rim and lifting and pulling the wheel till it slid off the studs and onto the ground behind his heels. The wheel was then dropped onto the ground with the lock ring side uppermost.

The valve was unscrewed with the valve tool and both were put in a pocket. If they were lost the whole exercise was wasted. Looking for them in the dust where you thought you'd put them could take half a day.

The lock ring was now sprung from its groove with the help of two, sometimes three, tyre levers leapfrogging around, one after the other, for the whole wheel. With one in each hand and using a foot to hold the third, middle one down, you had to be careful of it slipping and flipping up into the air. It could be dangerous. I know, because it happened to me once. My foot slipped. *Ouch. Damn.* The crossed eyes slowed the job somewhat. (A deep sigh and a drink out of the water bag was usual at this point.) Once the lock ring was off, it could be thrown aside with a sigh of '*I'm getting somewhere now.*' A lot depended on the length of time the tyre had been on the rim, or even on the surface of the rim where the tyre sat. Rust and dirt could clog everything.

Sometimes at this stage the tyre would be easily slipped off the wheel, but, if not, now came the big gun: the sledge-hammer. It had to have a long handle and to be very heavy. The hammer was raised above the head and with great force whacked down onto the wall of the tyre, slowly working all the way around till it was loose. It didn't hurt the tyre, but on a hot day it was tiresome.

Next, the wheel was turned upside down and sat upon some blocks of wood that were always carried in the toolbox, or if it was one of a pair of dual wheels then the other wheel could be laid upon the ground, proud side up, and the punctured bastard balanced on top. This allowed space for the top tyre to fall off the rim when bashed with the sledgehammer from the top side—again, a hot and tiresome job.

If it was still obstinate then dieseline kept in an empty peaches tin could be washed down around the rim where the tyre was jammed. This usually did the job with a couple more bashes from the hammer, although once or twice I had to bash a tyre off all the way down the rim. Bloody frustrating, tiring, and the air blue with curses. But with the proper heavy hammer and clearance it would come off. I can guarantee that.

Now we could get to the guts of the matter. The driver examined the tyre carefully, looking for a nail or whatever might have punctured the tyre, and if the problem could be seen he would remove it and then mark the wall of the tyre at that point and where the valve was positioned. There was a sleeve to be pulled out of the tyre first and then the tube itself. The tube was laid on top of the tyre, positioned by where the valve was, and this showed where the puncture was on the tube.

The puncture repair kit consisted of scraper, glue, patch—which was attached to a small metal-encased fuse—and clamp. The driver roughed up the surface around the hole, applied glue then placed the patch on top. He then applied the clamp to the patch case and folded tube as tightly as possible, pressing the patch firmly over the centre of the hole. He shoved a lighted match into the fuse, which burnt fiercely, producing the heat needed to weld the patch to the tube.

I usually waited thirty minutes before undoing the clamp. The tube was then fed back into the tyre, the valve screwed back in and the tube inflated just enough to have shape and no wrinkles, but soft enough to slip the sleeve back on inside the tyre.

Once the tyre had been eased back over the wheel and the valve stem positioned into its slot, the tyre could be lowered down into its place on the wheel. All that remained to be done was to hammer the lock ring back into place—with the join in the lock ring always on the opposite side of the wheel to the valve—and inflate the tyre to about 20 pounds or so—enough for it to expand and gently tighten itself to the lock ring. A few gentle taps with the hammer to the lock ring during this process ensured it was bedded properly and would not spring off as the air pressure increased.

It was important, when the driver was satisfied that all was ready for the tyre to be inflated, to check that the lock ring side was facing away from the driver or that the wheel was upside down, with the lock ring side underneath. Why? Because it had been known for a carelessly positioned or broken lock ring to spring off with the increased air pressure, with 70 pounds of air pushing it. I knew one driver who had both arms broken by a lock ring whipping off.

Maybe two hours was all it took, usually.

Where did we get the air from for the tube, out in the desert? Well, our old trucks didn't have air ride seats or air-conditioned cabs, but we did have a compressor attached to the gearbox with a long length of hose: with the motor idling it would pump more air than was needed for a 10 × 20 tube.

Repairing a tyre was just basic knowledge needed to venture out there into the desert. If you were unable to do simple repairs, you didn't belong in the big boys' playground.

6

Christmas refrigerators

I arrived at our Sydney depot, switched the motor off and pulled the handbrake on. It was just after 1 pm, a hot November day in 1956, one of those days that warn of a sizzling summer ahead. I had a feeling of uneasiness. There were no interstate trucks in the yard, empty or loaded—a bad sign for me. No trucks in the yard meant that any job that came up would be tossed my way. After the long, hot drive from Melbourne, I was intent on quickly emptying the cabin of my clothes and other odds and ends, then jumping into my car and like a flash of lightning disappearing out the gate and down to Bondi Beach for a surf. I had been dreaming of a swim all the way back from Melbourne. My new MG TD sports car was waiting there for me in the corner of the yard, and she was ready to go.

The MG TD: my pride and joy. She had imported Avon whitewall tyres and snakeskin seat covers.

Just then a window slid open at the office block across the yard and an arm waved at me urgently to come over.

Bloody hell, I thought. *Just my luck.* I threw an armful of clothes back onto the seat with disgust. Very reluctantly I ambled across to the window. The arm pointed to the office door. *I bet they want me to go down the wharf or something*, was my first thought, as I pushed the door open with a frown on my face.

The manager, Jock Paling, was all smiles. Now that was a warning if ever there was one: Jock smiling meant trouble. 'Good trip?' he asked.

'Yeah, no trouble. It's bloody hot out there today. I'm off to the beach,' I replied.

Jock pointed to a chair. 'Sit down for a minute, Ray. We have a problem and you're the answer.'

I sighed, looking up at the ceiling. *This'll be good*, I thought, grim faced. 'Go on,' I said to Jock.

'It's like this. Your truck is the only one of the fleet in Sydney.'

'So?'

'An urgent run has come up, really urgent, and I can't think of anyone better to get us out of this problem.'

'Bull.'

'It's right up your alley. The Nullarbor Kid to the rescue! But don't break down this time.'

'I'm going for a swim,' I replied, in a matter-of-fact tone.

'That's no problem. Go for a swim. Have a long swim—all afternoon. Be back here to load in the morning. For Perth.'

'*Perth?* Bloody hell, Jock, it's over a hundred degrees even *here* today. What's it going to be like out there on the Nullarbor Plain, that thousand miles of bloody goat track?'

'Can't think of a better team: the Nullarbor Kid and his Perth Express,' replied Jock. 'I'm sending a telegram to Perth today that Santa's Little Helper is on the way.'

The details of this bolt from the blue were as follows. The Sydney office of Mercury Transport, which had the contract to deliver President refrigerators, had been told that a load of refrigerators had to be delivered as soon as possible to the distant city of Perth. Rowley Goonan's electrical appliance

The Nullarbor Kid.

store in Fremantle, the ocean suburb of Perth, wanted to run a special Christmas sale promotion of the brand. For the sale and promotion to be a success, the refrigerators would need to be delivered and on the showroom floor at least two weeks before Christmas, and that didn't leave much time.

Mercury Transport was an innovative company back then. It specialised in transporting fragile goods, such as washing machines and refrigerators, uncrated over long distances. Thick canvas covers like sleeping bags were slipped over the appliances, which were then loaded handle to rear, tightly packed, with tarpaulins tied down over the load and wooden corner pieces on the outside top edge to allow each row to be tied by rope with two hitches, to keep the load from moving. It avoided the cost of wooden crates and was very successful, with no transport damage even over the Nullarbor Plain's rough gravel track.

Back in those days there were not many of us who took on the challenge of the Nullarbor Plain. I was one of the mad young adventurers who drove out there, but I wasn't too happy about being given this bloody load in the hottest part of the year, when the temperature was over 100 degrees Fahrenheit for days on end. I'd much rather have been surfing. But then, I had to admit, the money was good. I would need to leave within a week, allowing three weeks for the trip across in case of problems, which always reared their heads out in Never Never Land.

I went for my swim and all afternoon in the surf I thought, *Enjoy this, cos what's coming ain't gonna be good.*

•

Next day as scheduled the refrigerators were loaded and tied down. My frame of mind had swung from *Don't want to go* to *Okay, the money is good—let's do it.* I checked I had a couple of spare centre bolts for the trailer springs—one was sure to break before I returned to Port Augusta from the western bloody wilderness. And a few coils of fencing wire, just enough to tighten around splayed spring leaves if I ran out of centre bolts. A broken spring leaf could work its way out sideways and grind through the wall of the inside dual tyre; then the outside tyre, carrying all the weight, would eventually blow, so more trouble. I also checked I had a full toolbox.

I headed for Port Augusta, the last big town and the jump-off point to the west, by cutting across the lower part of New South Wales using the gravel road across the Hay Plains. That road was okay in the dry, but when it rained the plains turned into a black-soil bog that clogged up the wheels till they were jammed. A driver had to wait till everything dried out and then chip the mud off before he could start again. So when it was doubtful, it was the longer route, down through Victoria to join the sealed road to Adelaide. I was lucky this trip—no rain—so over the Hay Plains I went. The rain clouds thickened just out of Mildura, but I made it.

From the border with Victoria it was only a couple of hours across the top edge of that state to get into South Australia and safety. At the time, I was a wanted man in Victoria: they wanted the money or the body, preferably the money, which I didn't have, and the body wasn't too keen to go into Pentridge jail. I refused to pay road tax for using roads that most of the time were goat tracks. So there was a conflict of interests between the state and me that made life a continuing adventure when I roamed around in its territory. The border crossing was out in the country—no towns, just a signpost—and very seldom did the transport inspectors wait there. Too far to drag someone back to Mildura jail: they preferred to wait in town. But it was always a heart-pumping time as the border came nearer and nearer. Foot to the floor, much looking in the rear-view mirror, and I was across into freedom. Made it. I sang a little song, 'Ya missed me again, ha ha ha,' and lit a cigarette. Took them twelve years to catch me.

It was then an easy run to the top of Spencer Gulf, where awaited Port Augusta, the gateway to the west. It usually took a couple of days to fuel up, buy provisions and check everything, then double-check everything, and even sometimes check everything a third time. It was not the time or place to be in a hurry or forgetful.

While I was going through my checklist on the second day, a truck from the west trundled into town. It was splattered brown all over—mud had dried up over the headlights and windscreen—looking like a refugee from a war zone. It stopped across the road and the driver, Ron, climbed down then slowly walked across to where I was standing with a grease gun in my hand. I had just given the spring shackles another squirt of grease all round. Ron and I were not close friends but had crossed paths many times.

'Goin' west, mate?' he asked.

'Yeah. How's the track, Ron?' I replied.

'Bloody rough.'

'Where's the worst bits?'

'Its okay to Ceduna and Penong. Had some rain west of there, plenty of deep, muddy water sections over the road, some holes that deep and long I didn't think I would make it. One bit was about three trailer lengths. Stuck her in pit gear and just gave it to her, managed to slither and slide me way through, but I was worried there for a bit. The wind might have dried it out by the time you get there.'

A gravel section in the wet. The driver pulled off the road
for a quick cup of coffee—and it took half a day to
get back on the road again!

So, there had been rain out there, but it would take me at least five days, probably more, to reach the wet area, by which time it could have dried. The only roadwork done along the route was a grader twice a year, so in parts the road ended up lower than the surrounding countryside. Some sections were sandy and some hard rock, and when it rained the road became a canal for great lengths, some of which was impassable. Then the driver had to wait for it to dry before he could get through.

'Any loading in Perth to come back?'

'A bit around, a couple of trucks in town, but I didn't see anyone ahead of you on the way back here.'

'Thanks. I'm taking off at sundown—do the easy bit in the dark.'

'Good idea. Best of luck, mate.'

I sent a telegram to Perth advising I was leaving that night, and left Port Augusta as the sun was setting, as it was a thin, sealed road to the Iron Knob turn-off, which was where the road to the Golden West became a dirt track. But I soon stopped on the edge of the bitumen to have one last check around the truck with my torch. Kicked the tyres, tightened the ropes. All looked good. Always at this point I mentally ticked off the list for the last time—did I have everything? I forever had that feeling I had forgotten something.

I climbed back into the cabin and with the motor ticking over sat for a moment, smoking a cigarette, looking out through the windscreen to the end of the headlights' beam and thinking, *What am I doing here?* Then with a long sigh I put my left foot on the clutch pedal, changed into low gear, threw negative thoughts out the window, pressed my right foot down, brought my left foot gradually up, and away I went. Rattle, bang, up to second, then third, and into fourth, where it stayed, as fast as we could go on that stretch of road. Looking all the time from right to left at the track ahead, picking the smoothest parts and thinking, *Get your mind into gear, Ray. Nothing matters for the next week or more. To the west and back. Just find the smoothest way, okay?*

The hours dragged by, and at about 1 am I was getting a little tired; it was time for a sleep. I had to try to get going at dawn, before it became too hot.

The next day was a stinker—hot as hell. This part of the track had been dug up in the last rainfall and it took hours in second gear, the ruts were that bad. I opened the swing-out front screen, but the hot air rushing in was no help at all.

Eventually, I wandered into the little town of Ceduna, on the Great Australian Bight. It had taken two and a half days—not too bad. So far only a couple of punctures. I'd used two spares and had two to go, and then I'd have the long job of pulling the tyres off the rims and repairing any punctures I got after that. I bought another couple of tins of baked beans and a loaf of bread, topped up the water drum and took off again.

Penong Hotel—last beer before Norseman Hotel, Western Australia.
It hasn't changed much since the 1950s.

Penong was 45 miles further west, the very last bit of civilisation, with a shop, a couple of houses and a pub. It was getting towards sundown when I arrived, so a good time to stop till dark. Driving west into the sun for hours while looking for the smoothest parts of the track was very trying. The cracked windscreen sparkled in the sunlight, causing a perpetual frown on my face.

The beer at the pub was sold in tall bottles only. It was always too late to stop the barman opening another before you realised what he was doing, and so time went on. Eventually, reluctantly, I said goodbye to the barman and trudged up the dusty street to the wagon. I'd decided to drive on during the night for a bit and then camp till dawn.

It was 145 miles to Nullarbor Station, a sheep and cattle property that I had some mail for—the post office in Ceduna had asked if I would deliver it. That section took over three days, as I had nothing but tyre trouble all the way. I ran out of spares, so with the last two punctures I had to strip the wheels. Then there was a broken fuel line. To start with I couldn't find the leak that was sucking in air, but finally found it tucked under a part of the chassis that was hard to get at. I cut the offending part out and rejoined it.

I started coming across the few gates along the road that marked where the enormous properties on the plain joined. There was sometimes a sandy bog around them from vehicles stopping all the time. I would halt a truck's length back and walk up to the gate, swing it open, make sure it wouldn't move, then trudge back to the truck, roar through the sand in low gear to a truck's length past the gate, and walk back to shut it. Sooner or later someone would get bogged.

One night it was about midnight when I realised there was a gate due soon. It would be a good idea to park not far away on the other side, then if anyone came along they should be travelling slowly and I would not be a problem. That was a long shot, as no one in their right mind would come out here unless they had to, and we were very few.

I went through the gate and called it a night about 100 yards further on. After turning everything off I took the torch and the trusty .45 to have a piss. Why I didn't just open the door and wet the road I don't know. Anyway, I flashed the torch around on the ground beneath the door—all clear— and jumped down, wet the side of the road and wandered around the back of the trailer, constantly shining the torch on the ground all about me checking for snakes and any other strange things that might roam out here in the night. At the same time, I was checking the tyres and ropes. I moved up to the fuel tank, unscrewed the cap and shone the torch in to see the level. A quarter of a tank—plenty to get to Nullarbor Station before I swapped tanks.

I leant against the front of the cabin and clicked the torch off. I was amazed at the blackness. I looked around to discover if there was anything at all to be seen. Nothing—nothing but the bright stars. But, I must say, standing there all alone in the dark gave me the creeps. A shiver went up my spine. The loud, silent blackness was very unnerving. I started to think again about how I was out here all alone, no one for hundreds of miles, and that thought made me turn the torch back on, nervously sweeping the ground around me.

Suddenly, out of the darkness, there was a rustle in the bushes off to my left, or at least I thought it was a rustle. I froze for a second, petrified. Then I quickly swung the torch with my left hand, as my right hand and pistol followed at the same speed. Nothing there.

That's when panic gripped the intrepid adventurer, and I bolted for the driver's door as fast as I could, yanked it open, dived up into the seat, slammed the door shut and locked it. I turned on the headlights, pressed the start button, crashed into gear and off. Heart racing for no reason, eyes glued to the headlights' glow, fumbling for a cigarette. Santa's Little Helper was well and truly spooked.

I rattled on for half an hour, till I felt that whatever it was out there (or wasn't out there) was far behind. The imagination can play frightening tricks when it suits, believe me. I talked to myself—the brave overlander truck driver. 'Come on, there was nothing there.'

'Well, I didn't want to find out, okay? I like it in here with the door locked, so shut up.'

It definitely was a weird and forbidding place, and nighttime was the worst. I eventually talked the tough driver into stopping and having a sleep.

•

Next morning, the sun was up. I felt better, very brave, and it was not far to Nullarbor Station. The people at the station were lovely folk, couldn't do enough for us blow-ins, and they were happy to get their mail. I stayed overnight and took off at dawn. First, though, I kicked the tyres, checked the ropes, dipped the oil and added a little water to the radiator. As I left they called Eucla Station on their outback wireless set to tell Roy Gurney I was in the area. Although I had no mail for Eucla, at least they knew I was out there. That was a good feeling; someone knew I was roaming around. I would call in to see Roy, anyway.

The road in this section was so rough that I travelled for hours in third gear at about 15 miles an hour. I stopped at one of the water tanks out of curiosity, to see if there was any water in it. There was maybe a sludge in the bottom, but nothing came out of the tap. That was important information to tell anyone coming east. In all the years across there I never saw the tanks full. Sometimes they were half full, but mostly below that if there was anything in them at all.

Wandering cattle.

As well as cattle, which would wander across the track—always a problem—kangaroos were constantly around. About an hour after I left the water tanks I startled a 6-foot-high kangaroo, which then hopped down the road in front of me and left me way behind before he decided to veer off to the left. I poked my head out of the window and yelled at him, 'Come back, ya bastard! You're goin' too fast for me; I can't keep up.' I nodded to myself with a smile, wishing I could go as fast as that big roo. I hit the outside of the hot door with the palm of my hand with a laugh and gave him a wave as he hopped off into Never Never Land. As for me, rattle, bang, rattle, shake—that's all I had to show for my hot, sweaty effort.

'Talking to kangaroos now, I see,' I said to myself.

'Yeah. So what?'

The sun was like a ball of fire, a blow torch, that turned every bit of metal white hot. All I could do was keep squinting, looking for the smoothest bit of road, now and then wiping my face with a piece of towel. Then I remembered there was a bore pump around here somewhere. Bores were put down only in a few places, and the water was not drinkable, but I could have a shower and wash some of the grime off.

There it was, near another fresh-water tank.

The pipe stood quite high out of the ground, then bent at a right angle and ran horizontally for a few feet, and then turned another right angle and ran downwards for a couple of feet—like a small version of the early locomotive water pipes. A large wooden handle on the upright part could be vigorously moved back and forth and a rush of cold water would come pouring out. The only problem was if you were alone, with no companion to pump while you showered. It was difficult to pump and then jump the few feet or so to get under the water before it stopped. But, ever resourceful, we had over the years fixed the problem. An inner tube from a 10×20 tyre was cut in half. One end was slipped over the end of the bore pipe and tied to it, and a slit was made close to the other end, a small length of rope knotted through it, and—you beaut—you could stand at the pump and pull the rope tight, which moved the end of the tyre towards you, making the water come out in your direction.

You could feel it doing you good.

I was refreshed and going again, and my thoughts turned to what was going to happen next. It was always there, that thought of trouble circling around, like an evil something in the air just waiting to pounce. A few kangaroos off to the side looked at me with curiosity. They weighed up whether I was a danger and then, deciding I wasn't, continued eating.

•

Early afternoon. I was thinking I might stop for a quick check of the trailer wheels, and it happened. I heard a loud bang and knew another tyre had given up the ghost. I slowly rolled to a halt, knowing I was in for a lot of hard and hot work. I sat there for a bit, not wanting to get out into the boiling sun but at the same time knowing it had to be done. Damn and blast. This was the part I hated—and all nice and clean, too, after my shower. I was going to get hot and sweaty and very dirty.

It was too long to sundown and too hot to lie around waiting, so with a grunt I kicked the door open, swung around on the seat and pulled on my boots, grabbed my greasy, battered old stetson, shoved it on my head, leant over and plucked the belt and holstered pistol from the peg on the back wall and jumped to the ground, at the same time checking there were no snakes below.

I shoved a round up the spout of the pistol and walked carefully down towards the trailer wheels, all the time searching the ground around me for any hidden surprises. Then I laid the pistol in the shade on top of the wheel on the trailer rack. It would be easy to grab if I wanted it quickly. Another look around, wiped my face, settled the stetson firmly on my head and got to work.

Three bloody hours it took me. I couldn't get the tyre off the wheel. I had to soak the rim with dieseline three times and in between give it many bashes with the sledge-hammer before it gave way. That shower had been a waste of time.

The sun was disappearing as I put everything away, but it was still around 100 degrees. Enough was enough. I decided I would call it a day and get the primus going for a cup of black tea. Tea was the best thing—it makes you sweat and brings the body temperature down.

An hour later I decided to make a couple of miles and pushed on to a wider bit of track so as to be clear if anyone came along, not that it was likely. Hadn't seen anyone on the track for days.

After a good night's sleep—must have been at least eight hours—I stirred a little before dawn. It was bloody freezing. How could it be so hot in the day and so cold at night? Bloody no good, useless place. I lay there with the blankets pulled up to my neck, eyes closed, one voice telling me to get up and another saying to shut up and go back to sleep. 'Get up' won. I pulled my ex-army pants on, then boots and leather bomber jacket, grabbed the torch and tumbled onto the ground. With the primus pumped up and going, I put a can of water on to boil while I went around checking everything. No flat tyres, all ropes tight, oil okay, radiator okay, a can of peaches, a cup of tea and I was ready to roll.

I half sat on the front bar, leaning against the cab, and finished the first cigarette for the day watching the sun slowly light up the desert. I gave the track ahead a quick glance, not wanting to look at it yet—I'd be looking at it all day—stomped on the butt, swung around to climb into the cab, gave the front tyre a gentle kick to get her attention and said, 'Come on, old girl, be good for me today, will ya?' I think she heard, because I had a trouble-free run all day. Even sang a few songs and smiled a little.

•

I entered the state of Western Australia. There was no official government sign to mark it, only a pile of rocks and old blown-out tyres, various enamelled petrol and oil signs that were splattered with bullet holes, a post in the ground with a tyre hanging off it and a few messages left by early travellers. Some border! No one cared. Out here—yesterday, today, tomorrow, all the same.

Roy Gurney's place was down on the lower plain near the sea, surrounded by sandhills, just an old-fashioned wooden house built many years earlier. It was near the original telegraph station, a repeater station for messages between the east and west coast. The telegraph systems back then were not very powerful. The old sandstone building could be seen occasionally, when the wind blew the sand away, and then it would be lost for months, sometimes years, hidden beneath a sandhill or two. Roy's house was used by the telegraph staff way back when the repeater station was in use.

To get from the high plain down to the lower section, the road had been dug into the cliff face, no guard rail or fence, and, wonder of wonders, the mile or so was a sealed bitumen surface. I'd look at that beautiful bit of black road and think, *If only it was all like that across here.* But that was many years away in the future. I had to settle for this bit and another section up at Madura Pass, about 200 miles away, which took the traveller up onto the high plain again. They were the only sealed bits of road for hundreds of miles of desert. The reason they were sealed was that they were the only two sections in the one road across Australia that, if they eroded, could actually cause the road to close. And there was nowhere to detour. It was impossible to climb up and down between the high plain and the basin if those two sections fell away. So those two sections were sealed.

I always stopped at the top and gazed out to Roy's place in the far distance, marvelling at the scenery and thinking what a bloody big country this is. It was a good time to stop and check everything, and look down the cliff face. Little did we know back then that the Nullarbor Plain is riddled with underground caverns, some with water and others dry, a catacomb of unexplored phenomena that would be invaded by scuba divers in years to come. Unbelievable! Frank Lambert and I found an old abandoned homestead on one trip with a well in the forecourt. We threw rocks down but heard no splash; finally we tipped an old car axle down it and still there was no sound. Frank looked at me, I looked at him, and we took off, two very unsettled—no, two very *scared*—truck drivers. We didn't stop for the next four hours.

I decided to have a practice so grabbed the Winchester and took pot shots at a couple of tin cans someone had thrown out—all hits, no misses. *I'm still good*, I thought with a satisfied smile, then put it away. Back to work.

I slammed the ratchet handbrake off and rolled down to the bottom in third gear. Too soon, I was rattling and clanking once more on the corrugated track across the basin to Roy's house. He had a couple of hand-pumped petrol bowsers and always had some spare fuel available in 44-gallon drums.

It was only a short distance over the sandhills to the ocean. I was always going to go for a swim, but after a swim I had at Ceduna on one trip, when I went out in the bay where the

Eucla Pass.

great white sharks live and a 20 footer was seen where I had been swimming only a few minutes earlier, I sort of lost my urge for swimming in the southern ocean. Bore water was not as dangerous.

As I got closer I could see that the ruins of the old tele-graph station had emerged once more from the sandhills.

Roy heard me rattle up and wandered out. 'Anything for me?'

'No, not today, mate. No one loves ya,' I replied with a grin.

'Stoppin' the night?'

Roy Gurney's house, Eucla.

'Yeah, could do with a break. Hey, while it's still light, how about taking my photo? Me leaning on the wall of the old telegraph building. I have a camera somewhere here in the cab.'

'Sure, mate. Come on, the light's going quick.' Roy spun around, looking over towards the wall half-buried in the sand. 'The way the wind's blowing she could be gone soon, and who knows when she will reappear?'

I found the camera, a Kodak Box Brownie, and we hurried over the sand. That's the only photo I have of the old building—the one we took that day—although I was back and forth for years. But at least I got one photo of me with my cowboy boots, stetson and .45 Colt strapped on, standing beside a bit of history.

Old telegraph building, Eucla.

Roy was ahead of his time and had some metal badges designed with two holes at the edge that could be screwed onto a metal surface. They had a map of Australia in colour, with the words 'Trans Australian' at the top and 'Overlanders' below in a boomerang. They cost 75 pence. He sold them to the odd traveller. I purchased one, as the original I had on the front of the cabin had been stone-chipped. This one I wanted to keep at home as a memento for later years.

We had a meal and talked into the night, till I said I had better get some sleep. I said goodbye to Roy and hiked back to the truck, so if I wanted to go early I wouldn't disturb him.

He wanted a few supplies, like tea and sugar. I tucked the shopping list in my shirt pocket to give to the shop in Norseman, which would send the order by the first truck coming back east. It would probably take a week or two—it might even be me—but that was usual for out there. Norseman was still nearly 500 miles away, and who knew when I would get there and when someone would be coming back east? The few people who lived there knew how to spread their essentials with that sort of time lapse.

I was about halfway to the truck when Roy yelled, 'There's some rabbit trappers camped north of the road, top of Madura Pass. They're about twenty miles off the road. Look for a forty-four-gallon drum on the side of the road near some wheel marks heading north. They leave messages in it if they want any supplies.'

'Okay, will do,' I yelled back, trudging into the dark, flashing my torch on the ground ahead, not wanting to step on a Joe Blake. I climbed in and was asleep in minutes.

The 200 miles of road to Madura Pass were fairly easy, as it was all soft and sandy, not hard corrugation like the last few days had been. The biggest worry was wombat holes that the sand had covered over, but then, too late, there was a jolting lurch as the wheel dropped down and up again, the cabin complaining with squeaks and groans, me hoping it would

One of Roy Gurney's 'Overlanders' badges.

all hang together with no blowouts, and, even more important, hoping the steering wheel didn't break my wrist as it
whipped back and forth. Bloody holes, they were like snakes:
you couldn't see them till it was too late.

A few scrub turkeys ran across the road, but I knew it
was pointless to try to shoot one for a fresh meal: they were
always too quick. A flash of feathers and they were gone into
the scrub, completely camouflaged. I was lucky with a rabbit
sometimes.

The Madura Motel turn-off eventually came into view on
the left, away from the road some distance. It was a strange
place: a couple of buildings, one of fibro divided into a
couple of rooms with some iron-frame beds, some patched
and well-worn old lounge chairs, springs poking out of them
in all directions, on the shady verandah, and the other living

quarters for the people there and a tiny, sparsely furnished dining room—very plain and ordinary with a couple of tables. A traveller could get a meal there, but only during the motel's stated hours. If you were five minutes over the time advertised on the noticeboard at the door, no meal, no nothing. Hundreds of miles out in the wilderness.

There were a couple of fuel pumps—one diesel, one petrol—but you could never be sure if there was fuel available or even if they could be bothered serving customers. It was a strange place with strange people, and the American term 'motel' was a new word in the Australian vocabulary; we only knew about it from the movies. It was the only place I knew at that time that used the term. It was a large property, and the motel part was sort of added on, as they didn't really like or want visitors. I always wondered why they bothered with a dining room—they certainly were not friendly folk.

I'd had a run-in with them a year or two earlier and never went in there again. I had taken the mail and some supplies east from Norseman, arriving mid morning, and I got not a thankyou, not even the offer of a cold drink—it was as if it was my job to do these things for them when really I was doing them a favour. That was the last time I went in there, preferring to cook my own meals and sleep in the truck. A one-night stop there was too expensive, and the company wasn't the most pleasant. I think they had been out there too long and had lost the plot. Years later, when I watched the movie *Psycho*, Norman Bates's motel reminded me of the atmosphere in the Madura Motel—a strange place with strange people, and sort of spooky.

Anyway, it was getting dark. I chugged up the half-mile of the second bit of sealed track, the Madura Pass, looking for a 44-gallon drum on the side of the road. I mean to say, a brown 44-gallon drum out there in the brown desert at night, when it was as black as the ace of spades? What a laugh. Did they think I had X-ray vision? I started to weave back and forth so the headlights would pick up the edge of the road and a pace or two back from it. I decided I must have missed it somehow, when suddenly there it was, all by itself on the side of the track, and painted white! Easy to see. Brilliant.

I rolled to a stop, grabbed the pistol and torch, swung the door open, swept the ground below with the light and jumped down. I was very careful bending down to look into the drum, but no surprises. There was a note being held down with a small rock:

Please send to camp at top of Madura Pass.
2 cartons cigarettes
2 pkts tobacco and papers
Beer
6 Pr. Sox (black)
Whiskey
1 kerosene lamp
Tea
Kerosene (4 quarts)
Sugar

Matches (24 boxes)
Condensed milk
Lamp wicks (1 box)
soup
2 canvas water bags (carry type)
flour and anything else you think we need
salt
Baked beans
Irish stew
Send account to Commercial Bank, Norseman, for
payment.

I laughed at the priorities on the list: obviously, the top ones were the most important.

And that's how it was done back then. The various shops would send it all to the local service station, waiting for someone fuelling up to be going east who could take it, with directions to the drum on the side of the road. The shops would send their accounts to the local bank, which would pay them promptly, no questions asked.

I was in my shirt and shorts, shivering in the cold wind, so I grunted back to my feet and ran for the truck, tucking the note in my pocket. The Nullarbor Kid was the Nullarbor Postman as well. Part of being out there.

It was too windy to light a fire for a meal, and too cold, so I opened a tin of beans, sat in the cab balancing the tin on the steering wheel, used a soup spoon to gulp it down, the weak cab light on, looking out into the darkness and feeling cold and lonely. *Cold beans, cold night, black out there; bloody hell, think I'll call it a night.*

•

I woke at dawn. *How did it get so bloody cold?* Then, the morning pep talk. *'Get up.'*

'No.'

'Get up. Ya won't get to Perth on time this way.'

'Shut up.' A frown and a sigh. *'Okay, I'm getting up.'*

I struggled into my Second World War flying suit, pushed the starter button, as she ticked over ran around for a quick look, then jumped back into the cab, into gear and away we go. *Going to be windy today. Bloody steering wheel's cold.*

The road was fairly smooth here; I made good miles for an hour or two. The sun came up behind me—time for a warm breakfast. I rolled to a halt, switched off, opened the toolbox, grabbed the primus stove, pumped it up and soon the can of water was getting boiled.

Strange, you know—there was not a bloody person for hundreds of miles, but I still turned, pointed and pissed under the trailer. I could have signed my name in the dusty road for all it mattered, or waved it at the horizon; but no, hide it. Definitely creatures of habit, aren't we? I never could spell my full name when pissing in the dust. 'Ray' was no problem, but 'Gilleland' was always too many letters. 'Smith' would have been just right.

Okay, breakfast. Hot Irish stew, cup of black tea with two biscuits, second cup of tea while I had a bit of target practice with Betsy, as I called her, the .45 pistol. Gave her a clean, everything away, and here I go.

Then I started to notice the colour of the road was changing. The light bulldust sand, which was as fine as cosmetic powder and usually engulfed the truck all day if the wind was blowing the wrong way, was getting darker. That meant it was damp. Damp meant there was rain around. I looked up: blue sky, a few dark clouds, but still a bit cool. Not much point stopping to feel the dust and see how wet it was: keep going.

The road cut through low scrubby bushes; some could be called small trees. Up ahead I could see water—puddles here and there—not good. They were dangerous, as there could be wombat holes quite deep in that water, so it was best to try to dodge it. But then a sigh of despair: up ahead I could see that the whole road was one giant canal of dirty, brown, muddy water. Bloody hell. It looked to be four or five trailer lengths long, maybe 100 feet to the other end.

I knew what to do: I had done it many times. I eased up to the edge of the water, ratcheted the handbrake on and left the motor ticking over. I had discarded the flying suit earlier and had shorts and shirt on, driving in bare feet. I scratched around under the seat and found my 'water moccasins'—a pair of sandshoes. I slipped them on and grabbed a piece of old broom handle, about as long as a walking stick, that I kept in the toolbox for just such an occasion.

Off I splashed, walking along and poking the broom handle around, looking for deep holes under the water, all the way to

*The best way to invite trouble was to drive into water without checking
it out first. There could be anything under that water.*

the other end and roughly in line with where the driver's-side
wheels would come through, and then returning in line with
where the passenger-side wheels would be splashing through.
It was mostly between ankle deep and knee deep—seemed
okay. Solid enough, no deep holes.

There was one hole about halfway along on the left, but
it was off to one side. So I didn't drift into it I ripped a small
branch off a bush and poked it far enough into the muddy
bottom to hold, giving me a green leafy marker poking out of
the water. Sometimes you needed a few markers, and a straight
line through wasn't possible, making more of a zigzag. This
time there was no problem. But it told me that, as Ron had
warned me in Port Augusta, there had been rain out here. The
question was, how much? Was there more trouble ahead?

I scratched the back of my neck, looking up the road, thinking, *I need this like a hole in the head*. Anyway, I crawled through in low gear, noticed that my bow wave knocked the green bush marker over, but it didn't matter—I was through.

A few more long puddles and the track started to dry up—you beauty. A little further and I had left it all behind and was back to dry sand and corrugations.

A couple of hours later—surprise! In the distance (*Is it? Yes, it is!*) there was a truck coming. I couldn't pull over quickly enough. I had the primus out, the water on the boil, ready for a talk.

Then I recognised the red AEC truck. It rolled up, and there was a mate of mine, Dick Hurley. He was one of the two drivers I'd heard were in Perth when I was back in Port Augusta. As he pulled up, he yelled, 'G'day, y'old bastard!' with a big grin on his face.

'Well, look what the fuckin' cat dragged in,' I replied, with just as big a grin. 'I'm outta condensed milk, so ya'll hafta have it black, mate, okay?'

'I brought me own,' Dick replied, laughing. 'But if ya don't give any cheek I'll let ya have one spoonful, no more.'

Sitting in the dirt out of the sun under Dick's trailer we babbled on, asking this and that about loading, drivers and anything at all. We were both so happy to talk to someone. It was a welcome change from the monotony and lonesome existence with oneself out there.

Then all too soon it was time to part. I warned him about the water hazard down the road, and he filled me in about the road ahead. Dick had some supplies for Roy, so I told him to tell Roy I had the rabbiters' shopping list, if they contacted him.

'See ya, mate,' he called as he pulled away.

I gave a wave and watched his truck slowly get smaller and smaller, the two Fiat cars he had on board bouncing around, straining against the ropes holding them in place, and I felt quite lonely, thinking to myself, *Wish I was going that way with him.*

It didn't look too good for loading back to the east, if Dick could only get a couple of cars. *Oh well*, I thought, *anything can happen in the next couple of weeks. Let's get there first.* Santa's Little Helper put everything away and gazed back eastwards for the third or fourth time, but only seeing a small dust cloud now and feeling quite alone.

Okay, back to squinting into the sun. I thought I might run a little longer, into the night, make up a bit of time if the road was good. One last check around, then into gear and back to the grind.

I wanted to call in to Balladonia Station and see the Jackson family, so towards the end of the 90 Mile Straight—a section that was as straight as a gun barrel and whose surface was usually reasonable—I made camp for the night, knowing I could time it to get there in the morning. They were a nice family and I always enjoyed calling in. (I broke a camshaft in an Albion right in the middle of that 90-mile section on one trip going east. After fruitless attempts to get it going, thinking it was the timing chain, I drove it back to Sydney with only three cylinders working. All-up, the weight was over 30 tons. It was slow going, but the load was delivered—late, yes, but we got there.)

•

The following morning I was bad tempered. Maybe I'd been out here too long. Breakfast over, I looked down the track both ways—nothing. Not a bloody thing moved. I picked up a small rock and threw it at a bush, and missed. That made me pick up more and throw them angrily till I had hit the bush to my satisfaction. Bloody kid stuff. I wasn't happy, didn't want to be here. Bloody trucks, bloody refrigerators, bugger Perth, damn everything.

But there was no magic carpet out here to whisk me away, so I had to get on with the job. The usual check around, everything okay—I was thinking, *This is too good to last.* I decided to have a close look at the trailer springs, as I had been lucky so far. I hated spring and centre bolt problems. I grabbed a 7/8 ring spanner and rolled under the trailer axle to check the U-bolts. One needed a slight tighten; that was all.

Spanner and primus away in the toolbox, another look both ways down the track, then that 'must get going' feeling took over. I climbed into the cab, pressed the starter button and, while it built up air pressure, looked up the road ahead.

I rattled in to Balladonia Station homestead around midday. It seemed no one was about. I hollered and yelled, and went down to the sheep and cattle pens—no one. *Workers must be out there somewhere*, I thought, looking into the distance, *and the family must be in town.*

Okay, Norseman, here I come.

The next 100 miles were the worst of the whole trip, always a very slow part. The road was rock hard, and it had corrugations about 3 feet wide across the whole width of the road. The only thing was to put the driver's-side wheel onto the extreme edge of the road, which had a sort of gutter of soft sand, and rattle along till it was time to swap and put the passenger-side wheel in its gutter of sand. All the time the cabin and steering wheel were vibrating so bad that it was hard to hold on to the wheel. This went on for hours, and I always cringed on this bit of road, knowing what it was doing to the truck. It was a real nightmare. I could imagine nuts slowly unwinding and spring leaves flexing up and down, getting ever nearer to breaking point. The only thing to do was grit your teeth and keep going.

Suddenly, a roaring noise. The muffler had come adrift. It had to happen on this bloody bit of road. I clattered to a halt —the muffler had broken away from the tail pipe. Damn. Out came the roll of fencing wire. It was flexible enough to jam the pipe and muffler together, then I applied a tube of asbestos goo around the cracked section. I walked back to the cabin door, leant in and pressed the starter button, letting her tick over and dry the goo solid with the heat of the exhaust for about fifteen minutes. How long it would last was another matter.

The hours rattled by, and the little town of Norseman slowly emerged, backlit by the setting sun. I breathed a sigh of relief and relaxed as I hit the sealed road on the edge of town. The exhaust was a little louder, but who cared? A cold beer was close by. I gently eased her down the street to park near the hotel. A drink or two were definitely in order.

Norseman Hotel, 1956.

As I leant down to pull the throttle lever up, to cut the fuel off and stop the motor, I said, 'You did very well, old girl. Now, have a rest, while I have a drink.' I sat on the metal engine cover and dragged a not-so-dirty shirt from my bag and shook it out. Red bulldust filled the cabin like cosmetic powder—it could get in anywhere—but, no matter, I slipped it on, combed my hair, jumped down onto the road, this time not bothering to look for snakes, tucked the shirt into my shorts, rattled my pocket to check for money and I was off across that road as fast as I could go.

The worst was over. There were a few sections of dirt between the sealed bits up to Coolgardie, and then it was

400 miles of black bitumen to Perth. Nothing could stop me now—nothing.

Oh, is that beer going to be good.

It was a pleasant few hours, yarning with the locals over some drinks and answering questions about the Nullarbor Plain; not many there had ever gone more than a few miles east of town. There was nothing out there but trouble. That night I got the best sleep I'd had for days. I must have been very tired.

●

Next morning I had a bit of a headache—probably the way I slept. I delivered the shopping notes to the baker, who was up early, to pass on to the shops, and gave him some money to send a telegram to Rowley Goonan in Perth. A look around the truck (no pistol needed), no breakfast wanted, and I took off. Some Bex headache powder and a gulp of Coca-Cola, the wind blowing in the window, and I was a million dollars.

I drove through Coolgardie then pressed on to the little town of Southern Cross. The exhaust was getting louder. I didn't care. The wire would hold it together—sort of, anyway. A bit of noise was not going to stop me so close to the end. I had decided I would press on as quickly as possible, drive late into the night and be there first thing the day after next. I'd probably sleep a few miles short of Perth and arrive before all the traffic going to work.

As I found my way down to Fremantle, people were staring at this huge green monster of a truck, dried mud and dirt all over it, and making a very loud exhaust noise. The muffler was giving up the ghost, dangling by the fencing wire, but we had made it across without too much drama. The onlookers would have guessed where we'd come from by the dirty white New South Wales numberplates—they were few and far between in Perth in those days.

Suddenly, a fat man in shorts and singlet was waving at me from the middle of the road. I gave two pulls on the illegal air horns on the roof to say 'I see you,' and he ran for the footpath. Turned out he was the manager of the store and was showing me where I could park.

As I eased the truck into the gutter I noticed a couple more men in shorts and singlets waiting outside the store. I switched off, jumped down and walked around to meet them.

'Good to see you. How was the trip? You did well,' said the fat man. 'I'm the manager, Ken, and this is Bill and Jim. We've come in early to help unload and get the refrigerators into the front window and onto the shop floor.'

I smiled as I shook hands with them all, glad to finally be there.

'Come on, boys, undo the ropes and let's get started,' Ken said, moving towards the nearest rope.

'You're going to get very dusty and dirty, you know,' I said.

'Our good clothes are in the back of the store; that's why the shorts and singlets. We have a shower in back, and George and Sam are inside changing. They'll be out in a minute.'

Well, this is going to be good, I thought to myself. I'll be unloaded in no time.

It was about 8 am. We undid the ropes and pulled the tarps off onto the road, and I showed the boys how to fold and roll them into a bundle. There was dust going everywhere, clouds of it, rolling down the street, but the boys were not worried; they seemed to enjoy it all.

There was about 12 inches of floor space at the back of the truck, and I scrambled up and slid one of the heavy green covers off the refrigerator nearest the gutter. Ken and Bill reached up as I tilted it over, and Jim waited to grasp the top, then slowly they lowered it to the footpath.

George and Sam had brought out a fridge trolley, which they slipped under the refrigerator. They wheeled it down the path to the corner of the shop, where there was a hose attached to a tap. George grabbed the hose, turned on the tap and started to spray the refrigerator with water, then Sam whipped the door open and George pulled all the packing out, tossed it to one side and sprayed the inside as well. They then wiped it down inside and out, put all the shelves and crisper drawers back in and wheeled it onto the showroom floor. It looked as if it had just come off the assembly line at the factory. If you were needing a refrigerator that Christmas time, well, there it was.

That was how it went: refrigerator tilted over, down onto path, wheeled away, hosed and wiped down, and into the store. We were going like clockwork when I suddenly spied a well-dressed elderly couple standing at the edge of all this activity, watching with interest.

'Ken, I think that couple want to get past,' I said. The footpath was full of refrigerators, and water was running everywhere.

'No, that's Mr and Mrs Pearson, our first customers for the day,' Ken replied. 'Good morning! Well, they are here,' he called to them, pointing at the refrigerators scattered around. To me, he continued, 'They are here to buy one of the fridges. They've been waiting for you to arrive, ringing every second day to get a report on how you were progressing.' He called out again to the Pearsons, 'Go on in. The boys will look after you.' They negotiated the hive of activity on the footpath and disappeared into the store.

I noticed the front window of the shop. Half of it was bare, just a large black-and-white paper banner hung diagonally that read:

A NEW REFRIGERATOR for CHRISTMAS
Order now.
Guaranteed delivery.
Truck load leaving Sydney this week.

Below that was a smaller banner giving a date and:

The truck is at PORT AUGUSTA.

Another hung below that, with a later date and:

It made it to NORSEMAN!

Finally, another banner, written in larger letters:

REFRIGERATORS HERE TOMORROW!
Come in, order now.
Not many left.

Wow, I thought, this is unbelievable. Everybody knew where I was most of the time, except me.

Apparently, there had been advertising in the newspapers for weeks about this load. More and more people started to appear. Some were threading their way through the water and refrigerators on the footpath. Others, having made their purchase, were off home to await delivery. The shop was frantic, people coming and going everywhere. George had left Sam to clean the refrigerators and ushered in those standing around to show them the goods and sign them up. Home deliveries would start that afternoon. It was showtime in Perth.

There were only a few left unsold by the end of the day, and they went quickly. For poor old Perth, the most isolated capital city in the world, this delivery was big news.

The unloading was finished by 10.30 am. I gathered the tarps back onto the truck, tied them down, ready to go. Leaning on the trailer gunwale with my chin on my folded arms, watching all this activity across the empty deck, pictures of the trip flashed through my mind. I thought, *They have no idea what it took Santa's Little Helper to get those refrigerators here.* The dirt track, the loneliness, the cold, the tyre troubles, the scary parts, the boredom, the whole bloody thing. And the heat! That was the worst: it sapped your will to keep going. I let out a long sigh and smiled to myself. *Oh well. Next problem: repair the exhaust, get a service for the truck, and can I get a load back to the east coast?* My spiffy MG roadster was waiting back home to take me surfing.

Turning to leave, I shouted a general goodbye, was waved at briefly in return, everyone far too busy to stop and say thanks or well done: there were refrigerators to be sold and delivered. My delivery docket had been signed—clear and no damage—so that was that.

The Subiaco Hotel, where I usually stayed when in Perth, was calling. My very noisy exit was not noticed by a single soul. Cars and people everywhere, all converging on Rowley Goonan's electrical appliance store. My job was done. There were refrigerators in Perth for Christmas.

7

Ken Grey

Ken was a character. He was small—about 5 feet 5 inches—and never wore shoes, winter or summer. His feet were as hard as nails; they were so callused he could walk on broken glass and crush it as if he were wearing shoes. His only work clothes were a shirt and shorts, no matter what the weather.

In around the late 1950s, when he was twenty-four or so, he came to work for Jack Seaton's Transport. He was given an AEC Monarch in Seaton's colours, red and black, to drive. One Monday morning he took on a full load of car batteries from the Exide factory at the bottom of Taverners Hill, Petersham, in Sydney, for delivery to Exide in Adelaide, over 1000 miles away. A layer of batteries were floor-loaded one by one, by hand, to fill the trailer, and then a few extra rows, one or two on top, above the axles, usually made it about legal. A sheet of crinkled cardboard was laid under the rows that were stacked higher and proved an ideal insulation, as the batteries themselves were heavy and, once tarped and roped down, never moved.

Now this trip started okay. Ken was given his expenses— money to buy his meals with—and off he went down the Melbourne road, then across the dry Hay Plains into South Australia.

On the second night, sometime after midnight, he was on a long, gentle downward slope near the town of Morgan. Ken wanted to be in Adelaide when the factory opened that day, and he was nearly there. But he lost it—maybe a nap at the wheel—and the truck left the road, crashed through a fence, and over she went: batteries flying everywhere, all over the paddock.

Ken wasn't hurt, only a few bruises; he was lucky. The Monarch had rolled, but ended up on its 'feet', so Ken decided the only thing he could do was reload the batteries, one by one, and get it all back to Sydney, and he did just that. The truck was a mess, but he got her home, load and all. As Jack said to someone, 'How could you fire him after he had done that?' And he didn't fire him. Could you imagine doing that today? Transport inspectors and the police would be hysterical.

*Ken Grey's battered Monarch at Jack Seaton's Transport yard at the
Sydney haulage terminal. The drum on the right was used in the open
shed in winter for heating, as the mechanics sometimes worked on the
trucks till after midnight while the drivers waited for the okay to go.
In the background are two Mercedes-Benz 315 models in the Cooper
Barnard colours, before they were painted in Jack Seaton's colours.
One 315 with general loading can be seen behind the Caterpillar grader.
(Seaton's had the Caterpillar contract from the Melbourne factory.)
There is a car-carrier trailer on the right. Above the Monarch's cabin in
the background is the early Mascot airport. The planes came very low
over the yard when landing. It is now Sydney's International Airport.*
(Courtesy Terry Gordon.)

8

Yesterday

I was helping out on a furniture-removal van as a casual offsider. There were two of us plus the driver, delivering a house load of furniture that was a day late on its trip from Sydney to Southport. Sometimes on long-distance removals a hold-up would occur, but we were expecting an unhappy reception, as the office hadn't informed the waiting homeowners.

As we drove up the street and passed the house we could see a lady standing on the front porch, watching us with a grim look on her face.

I said, 'Don't look too happy, boss, does she?'

'Nah, she'll be okay,' he replied.

He backed into the drive, and we got out and opened the back doors. The lady was still on the porch, standing with arms folded and a look that could kill. The driver hopped up into the van as we unwrapped the furniture and grabbed a dining chair. He started to carry it up the path, at which point the lady angrily started to walk towards him.

They were only a few feet away from each other when the lady stopped, put her hands on her hips, and shouted, 'Where have you been? You should have been here yesterday!'

The driver, quick as a wink, put the chair down, sat on it, facing her, and with a very concerned look on his face said, 'Why? What happened?'

The lady's eyes nearly popped out of her head. She hesitated, then turned around and stormed back inside the house. The driver winked at us and followed her with the chair.

We unloaded as quickly and quietly as possible. The lady didn't say another word all the time we were there; she just glared at us whenever we entered the house. There definitely weren't going to be any tips from this job.

Anyway, we laughed all the way back to the depot. He was a cheeky bugger, that driver.

Ron Burrows

9

A wet step on a wet night

On the old Pacific Highway between Brisbane and Sydney, just north of the little town of Bulahdelah, is a place called O'Sullivans Gap. It is on a section of road that winds its way along the edge of the Great Dividing Range, and a steep climb. Coming from the north in the old trucks it wasn't too bad, but southbound it was a steep and long uphill grind before the easy downhill run into the township.

The name 'highway' implies a four-lane divided road, but that was not the Pacific Highway of the 1950s. Back then it was a narrow, sealed macadam strip with just enough room for two trucks to pass without colliding. There were many long gravel sections plus four ferries—some large, some small— that crossed the main rivers along the road. It would be hard to rate it even as a secondary road today.

One of the four ferries on the Pacific Highway to Brisbane.

Southbound, climbing up Sullivan's was a good chance to fiddle with the radio to see if a station could be found. Radios were primitive, and the radio stations very underpowered. A long-distance driver was always looking for and then losing stations—most annoying when a popular song from the hit parade faded to nothing but noisy static. Then it was twist, fiddle, still nothing, damn, switch it off. One night around midnight I turned the radio on for fun: crackle, static, and then, lo and behold, I heard Bing Crosby singing. I couldn't believe it. It turned out it was a radio station in Singapore. It only lasted a few minutes, then I lost it.

On a trip in 1954 Jim Boler was driving for Parsfield Transport, an International 190 with a tandem trailer. It was early morning, about 2 am, with Jim relaxed and a little sleepy, climbing up Sullivan's Gap in low gear, all-up weight 25 tons or a bit more. The trailer was tarped down neatly and everything seemed to be A-okay in Jim's world, except for the poor radio reception. The 190 had never let him down and always did what was expected of her—a great truck.

The headlights' glow lit up the wet road ahead; it had been raining on and off all night, but the cabin was warm. Jim reached for the half-empty bottle of lemonade. A couple of gulps reminded him he needed to have a pee. But he couldn't stop where he was, as the road was too steep to take off again. (It always happens at the wrong time and the wrong place, doesn't it?)

Then, on an impulse, with what he thought was a brilliant idea, he pulled out the hand throttle on the dash a couple of notches, fiddled with it a bit to get it just right, and the old girl settled into a nice rhythm at about 4 miles an hour, plodding her way up the hill and no foot needed on the pedal: she could do it all by herself. Jim waited a minute just to be sure his idea would work. Everything was okay. Jim smiled smugly. *Now I'll open the door, stand on the step and wet the road—simple! Problem solved. No downtime needed at the top to pull over and stop.* At this point the rain had eased to a drizzle, so Jim knew he wasn't going to get too wet, just a little damp, while standing out there on the step. A quick scan of the road ahead, another check of the dimly lit gauges—hearing the normal motor noise, Jim thought everything seemed spot on—so with a quick jerk of the handle he pushed the driver's door open, at the same time twisting around to climb down onto the wide metal step.

As Jim's foot touched the wet step it instantly slipped off it, and he was catapulted down onto the road a good 6 feet from the drive wheels as they slowly but surely rolled up the hill past him, into the darkness. He lay there on his back for a split second in disbelief. *What happened? What am I doing here?* It was all so quick, his thoughts were muddled. Then, next instant, his mind was telling him something else as the 190 trundled on up the hill. He was in big trouble if he couldn't get back in that cabin.

The fall had knocked the wind out of him momentarily, and at the same time his bladder had let go, which had been the whole purpose of this exercise, so something had been accomplished. But the 190's driver's door had banged shut and she was plodding up the hill unaided, not needing Jim, and going well—actually, too well, as she would reach the top any minute now, and then what? Pictures flashed through Jim's mind of him chasing the 190 down the other side of Sullivan's Gap into the township of Bulahdelah, knowing he couldn't catch her. He didn't have another moment to lose; he had to catch her and get back in behind the wheel before all hell broke loose.

He scrambled to his feet, but then slipped again: his leather shoes were like rollerskates. A common tree in the Australian bush is the eucalyptus, and when it rains the water washes slippery gum to the ground from the eucalyptus's leaves. In a certain light it can be seen as an oily-coloured substance, but

Jim's problem was that he couldn't see the slippery patches. By this time the trailer wheels were rolling past him and he saw he was getting left behind; the rear of the trailer, all lit up with its red lights and white numberplate light, was slowly but surely getting away.

He started to run uphill after the 190 while all sorts of mental pictures continued to run through his head—the truck would be wrecked, maybe half the town would get demolished, he would lose his job, he would be the laughing stock of the road, how could he explain how it happened? Then panic gave wings to his feet and he took off like an Olympic runner.

Huffing and puffing, slipping now and then, catching his balance, slipping again, he was just gaining on it. He was up to the drive wheels and thinking, *Be careful! Don't slip over now.* Then, with a lot more huffing and puffing, a slip and a slide here and there, he made it to the cabin.

Still running hard he reached up, pulled the door open with one hand and made a grab for the steering wheel with the other. He missed, but one hand had grabbed the inside door handle—that helped—then with a hop and another couple of quick steps on the road he heaved himself up, grabbed the wheel this time, and with a superhuman yank and kick he was back in the seat where it had all started about sixty seconds earlier.

The driver's door had banged shut again, this time with Jim inside. Breathing hard but once more behind the wheel, he gave a shudder: the adrenalin was still pumping. He let out a long sigh of relief and stared at the road ahead, but this time his eyes were glazed—he couldn't believe what had happened. In the meantime the 190 was completely ignoring him, still chugging up the hill as she was supposed to do, as if nothing had happened and he wasn't needed.

He waited a couple more seconds, sitting there wide eyed and staring out into the headlights' glow, then, with a shake of his head and with his foot on the pedal once more, Jim smacked the hand throttle in and relaxed a little, everything familiar and back in its place. He wiped down his wet shirt and pants with his hands, at the same time wondering which wetness was which . . . It would be quite a few hours down the road before any place would be open to have a wash, and by then it wouldn't matter anyway. He gave another long sigh of relief and scratched around looking for a cigarette and that bloody lemonade bottle again.

Ever tried running uphill beside a truck? No? Don't ever try it. After that night, Jim was always extra careful to hold on to the door very firmly as he stepped down onto what could be a wet step. Whenever he decided the road needed wetting again on a steep uphill climb, that is.

10
Trees and needles

He was of medium height, slim build, olive complexion, brown hair and about twenty-three years old. Born during the Depression and grew up during the Second World War. Missed being called up for war service by a couple of years. First truck he drove was a Thames Trader for Westcott Hazell in Sydney, in 1948. He had always wanted to travel and found interstate road transport just the job. Good natured, did his job without fuss, liked his bosses, looked after his trucks and tried to keep out of trouble. The last part was hard, as when he graduated to long-distance trucking trouble always seemed to find him in this game of cat and mouse with the different state governments' road transport regulations.

In the winter of 1954 he was in Melbourne. He had just loaded three Standard Ten car bodies on the top deck of the 1954 AEC Matador car carrier he was driving and a couple of drive-on Standard cars on the bottom deck, then was told he had to leave immediately, up over the mountains to Sydney, nearly 600 miles away, to be unloaded and ready to load late the next afternoon for an urgent run to Brisbane.

Progress had been made from the early pipe-frame double-deck car carrier trailer to a heavy all-steel trailer that could carry cars as well as white goods (refrigerators, washing machines and the like) when needed. He had already complained that he had no trailer brakes working and wanted them fixed before he left Melbourne. It was dangerous driving with no trailer brakes, but he was told to take it easy, just get there, and the brakes would be fixed before he left for Brisbane. His was the only truck that could be available to load in Sydney the next day, and the customer could not be let down.

He shook his head, thinking, *Wintertime, plenty of rain around, maybe even some ice and snow up the road.* He didn't like it one bit, but, *Oh well, here goes.*

Trying to hurry along Sydney Road on the way out of Melbourne at about 11 am on a busy Thursday was hell. Every major intersection's traffic lights had a large clock-like hand that was always just into the yellow zone, ready to hit the red 'stop' mark as he approached, or a tram was setting down passengers and then taking off, leaving him too little room to get past. He had that sinking feeling: the trip was going to be trouble. How right he was.

Finally he shook the city off, climbed Pretty Sally, the hill out of Melbourne, and started to feel he was making some headway. It was going to be a long night with very little rest, as he had to be unloaded by noon the next day in time to load for Brisbane as quickly as possible and then have the brakes relined. The top speed for the AEC Matador was 42 miles per hour, which meant driving all night with only a couple of naps.

The run up through Victoria to the New South Wales border was a piece of cake, usually about four and a half hours, mostly flat, an easy road, and he could take it quietly through the towns, where the truck brakes only were needed, not the trailer brakes. After topping up the fuel tank at Joe's Service Station in Wodonga, on the Victorian side of the border, he left Albury, on the New South Wales side, around 4 pm to face the tough up-and-down road through the mountains to Sydney. Being winter, it was dark early, and, worse, there were rain clouds around; in fact, in sections the road was still wet from showers that had passed through earlier, and it was bloody cold, a freezing wind blowing through all the holes in the cabin. He decided to stop for a meal at Tarcutta, about 140 miles up the road—should be there about 7.30 pm, though maybe it would take a bit longer with no trailer brakes and rain threatening. The cafe would still be open even if he was a little later than 7.30. He looked forward to playing the jukebox while waiting for the mixed grill to be served. They dished up a good meal there. His favourite tune at the moment was The Chordettes singing 'Mr Sandman'.

The pub was open at Woomargama, but he didn't stop and took it carefully down the hill. He tried the trailer brakes a couple of times—nothing, absolutely nothing. It didn't make for a comforting feeling, knowing he was pulling a heavy double-deck trailer with only the prime mover brakes and nothing to help him in an emergency. He was well aware of the danger of having no trailer brakes. With the sudden application of the prime mover brakes without trailer brakes, the weight of the trailer would push the prime mover sideways into a jackknife, completely out of control, and he could end up anywhere.

It started to rain coming into Holbrook, a quiet little town but with nowhere to eat. It got even colder as well, so just on the edge of town he stopped at the side of the road and ran around, kicked the tyres—all okay—then pulled on his wartime flying suit—not the usual blue nylon type that many drivers wore but a brown furry one he had bought at an army disposals store a couple of years earlier. Everyone laughed at him, said he looked like a big brown bear. They might laugh; he was as warm as toast in it despite the freezing-cold wind in the cabin. There were even times up in the high New England Range that he had to wear kangaroo-skin mittens as well as a leather flying helmet. Air-conditioning and heating were all by natural means in the 1950s: cold air blew through the cabin in winter, and hot air was there to be enjoyed in the summer. Wonderful arrangement. He plodded on, up through Little Billabong towards Kyeamba.

There was a fairly steep drop down into a little valley,

and he was quietly letting the weight of the motor hold it back, travelling maybe 30 miles an hour. The rain was pouring down, the little wiper trying its best to keep the water off the screen. He had just turned the headlights on when he saw ahead of him, and taking up the whole road, a bunch of cattle, about seven or eight of them. Some were wandering up either side of the road, but three were smack bang in the middle. With the poor penetration of the headlights through the downpour he was onto them without warning, and at the same time he was saying to himself, 'They shouldn't be out here on the road, and even worse at night, and bloody hell the road will be slippery with the rain . . . What's going on?' All too late. Within a split second, while taking this all in, he had rammed on the trailer brakes for all they were worth and gingerly touched the brake of the prime mover, a pick between having a thousand hamburgers on the hoof through the windscreen or hoping he could dodge them.

Everything held for a few seconds and then it was too much: the weight of the trailer took over, pushing the cabin sideways to the left, the usual jackknife position, and all he could do was hang on to the steering wheel like grim death, being propelled sideways off the road at speed into the trees. One mighty-big eucalyptus got in the way, and the cabin, with the driver's door now travelling at the front, slammed into it, uprooting the tree. The prime mover came to a halt, straddling this huge tree trunk, which had sheared off above the cabin; the upper trunk fell on the roof and rolled off.

With the force of the impact, his head had snapped sideways, shattering the driver's-side window, and while the glass was still all there in place, it was now a spider's web of cracks. His head felt funny, dead-like. Everything was in darkness, but the motor was still ticking over, having missed the impact because the driver's side of the cabin had taken the full brunt of the collision. Half of the windscreen had fallen out, and rain was blowing in over him.

He sat there, a little dazed, trying to get his thoughts into gear. It was then that he felt a wetness oozing down his face. He touched the top of his head but it seemed to have no feeling. He was just deciding to do something when he heard above the sound of the motor a voice calling in alarm. 'Hey, mate, hey, are you okay?' A face was there in the darkness, next to the shattered window, trying to see in—just a dark shadow.

It turned out it was his mate Garry Freeman, trying to open the door, which was buckled inwards and wouldn't budge. Jumping down off the fallen tree trunk Garry ran around, scrambling over the branches, to the passenger side, reached in under the side of the cabin and yanked the fuel rack arm back to stop the motor. He then jumped up, pulled the passenger door open and clambered across the seat and up onto the cover over the motor that divided the driver and passenger seats.

The driver looked sideways at him then said, very slowly and very angrily, 'Did you see those bloody cows out on the road? The bastards. I'm goin' to shoot them.'

'Never mind the cows. Are you all right?' Garry asked quickly.

'I think so. My head's numb, that's all.'

'Have ya got a torch?'

'Yeah, somewhere. Maybe on the floor.'

'Can you move your arms and legs?'

'Yeah, they're okay.' The driver slowly stretched his arms and shuffled his feet.

'You've got blood all over your face. Where's it coming from?'

'I don't know. What blood?'

'Running down your face.'

'Oh, that. I don't know. I thought it was rain,' the driver said, wiping his head, looking at his bloody hand.

Garry peered closer and could see that there were small amounts of blood spurting up into the air at regular intervals from the top of the driver's head. 'Your head's bleeding, ya dopey bastard. Ya must've smacked it on the window.' Garry fumbled around, looking for something to put on the driver's head. He grabbed a pair of white woollen long johns that were with the other scattered clothes that had toppled out of a bag to the floor and plopped them on the driver's head. 'Put your hand up there and press down tight.' The two white legs hung down like long pigtails. They looked funny, but that didn't matter—there were no more spurts of blood, so the bleeding seemed to have stopped. 'Okay, listen, we're well off the road—everything will be safe. We'd better get you into Tarcutta to the doctor's. I think ya might need some stitches in your head.'

'We'd better check everything first before we leave,' the driver said slowly.

'Yeah, yeah, come on, out this side. Hurry up.'

'I'd better pack my bag and stuff, and take the tools under the seat.'

'Bugger the bag and tools. Just get out, come on.'

'All right, all right, I'm coming. Hey, wait on—check my forty-five is in the bag and find my rifle; it's behind the seat. I'm gonna shoot some of them bloody cows before we go.'

'Never mind the bloody cows; they're long gone. I saw them galloping up the road at a hundred miles an hour.'

'Damn. Bring the rifle anyway—might get one of them on the way. Don't want to leave it behind.'

'Yeah, okay, come on. I'll help ya down.'

As the driver crawled out from behind the steering wheel and over the engine compartment, he asked, 'Anyway, where did you come from? I didn't see you anywhere back there.'

'I've been chasing ya from Albury. I was fuelling up when ya went past. I knew you were up ahead but I didn't think I would find ya tree loppin'.'

The driver climbed into Garry's truck and they were off. It was only about 20 miles to Tarcutta. Slowing down across the creek bridge at the south of the town, Garry said, 'I'll wheel into the pub and ask if there's a doctor in town.'

'Now that's a good idea, and we can have a drink to celebrate a lucky escape.'

'That might not be a good idea. Doctor and police station,

Tarcutta Hotel, 2009.

in that order. You to the doctor, and me to report the cattle out on the highway.'

'Okay, but I'll come in with ya. I need a piss.'

There were not many in the bar, and the few that were there took a good look at the two blow-ins. They must have looked strange together. One was normal, in a heavy leather jacket and corduroy pants, but the other was a sight to see. Brown, furry flying suit with what looked like a white, blood-splattered turban with a long, white pigtail hanging over each shoulder, one arm bent upwards, holding on to the top of the turban, and dried blood all over his face as if he had been in a fight. The locals didn't get many strange sights

105

in a little town like Tarcutta, and to see this pair emerge out of the night and make for the bar was indeed a talking point.

Two beers were ordered, and the turbaned one moved on to the toilet.

'What happened to your mate?' the barman said.

'Some cattle on the road back near Kyeamba. He tried to dodge them and ended up in the scrub, knockin' trees down,' explained Garry. 'Any doctors in town? He needs some stitches, I think.'

'A new one just arrived a couple of weeks ago. Up the hill a bit, and the brown house over on the right.'

'Any police over at the station this time of night?'

'He's out of town, back later tonight.'

'If ya see him before we do, tell him there's a bunch of cattle loose about 20 miles out towards Kyeamba.'

Turban head came back to the bar and finished his drink. 'My shout and we'll go,' he said.

'Come on, we'd better get ya to the doc's,' Garry replied.

'No, I'm having my shout. Fill 'em up again, thanks,' he said to the barman.

So time went on and drinks were downed till even the barman said, 'You had better go: there's blood all over my floor.' The pigtails were dripping a little.

Deciding to book a room for the night at the hotel, after ringing the boss they trudged up the hill. After bashing on the doctor's door and a lot of yelling, they heard a shuffling sound and a light went on, the door opened and a young fellow with thick glasses looked out. 'Yes?' he said, and then seeing the turban and pigtails waved them inside. The door closed behind them and the young doctor shuffled after them. Poor fellow had a club foot as well as thick glasses.

After being told what had happened the doctor unwound the turban, which by now had well and truly stuck to the driver's head, and said, 'Hm,' peering closely. 'Yes, some stitches needed there.' He washed the wound in between spurts of blood and then told the driver to keep pressure on the wound with his two fingers on a small gauze pad, as it kept spurting with a regular rhythm any which way.

Then, right in front of the worried driver, he started to thread a large, curved needle with cat gut. He had a little trouble threading it while adjusting his thick glasses, which kept trying to slide down his nose.

Looking at Garry and the doctor, his eyes constantly swivelling back and forth, the driver loudly asked, 'How about while he is getting ready we slip down the pub and have a quick one?'

'No,' said Garry firmly. 'You just sit there and shut up.'

All eyes were focused on the needle threader, willing him to succeed. At last he did it.

Next came the hypodermic needle—it looked big enough to put a horse to sleep. He moved behind the driver and said, 'I'll just put a little deadener up there so I can put a few small stitches in place, and that will be it.'

A few small stitches, the doctor said. The driver thought the needle looked big enough to sew up a wheat bag. But he cleared his throat, shuffled his feet a little, looked at Garry and decided to be brave. He didn't feel the injection—that was good—and then he was told to move his fingers slightly so the stitching could start. Little by little his fingers moved along as the gash slowly closed.

'Okay,' said the doc. 'Take your fingers away.'

Lo and behold, right in front of his eyes there was blood spurting regularly onto the floor.

'Hm. Looks like we have to put the stitches closer together,' said the doc, dabbing at the small fountain. 'A couple of veins there are being a bit of a nuisance.' He walked over to a cabinet, opened a drawer and took out what looked to be a large pair of wire-fence cutters; or that was what the driver thought— he had a pair like that in the toolbox. After a few snips and a new pressure pad applied by the driver's two fingers, another intense battle ensued with the needle and gut. This time when he took his fingers away it was down to an oozy dribble. 'Okay,' said the doc. 'We'll get it this time.'

While all this was going on the police constable had arrived. He took all the particulars and said he would look into it, and then left, never to be seen or heard from again. He wasn't about to upset a local farmer over a few cows.

A third try resulted in no fountain, not even a dribble. Hooray! 'I'll just put a piece of gauze over it to keep it clean. Go to your local hospital in ten days; they will take the stitches out,' said the doctor, with what sounded like relief in his voice.

Thinking of getting back to the pub for another nightcap before it shut, the driver didn't notice that the 'piece of gauze' was a huge, pink Elastoplast bandage that stretched from his left jawbone over the top of his head and down to the right jawbone, covering both cheeks, with splits in the sides to let his ears poke out like one of Santa's elves. There was a scraping of chairs and a hasty retreat to the pub, just in time to down a few more.

With a slight headache the next morning—due to the accident, naturally, and not the nightcaps—the driver made arrangements for the truck to be towed home and for the load to be transhipped. Fortunately, there was not too much damage to the cars, as the trailer had stopped upright.

Ten days later the driver arrived at St George Hospital in Sydney to have the stitches out.

'What happened to you?' asked the nurse.

'Truck accident out in the bush—a few stitches to come out,' the driver said.

'A cut with a few stitches?' she laughed. 'I thought you'd had brain surgery, with all that Elastoplast up there. Wasn't there a doctor in the town, only a vet? Hey, everybody, look at this!' she called out.

All of a sudden he was surrounded by nursing staff making comments like 'You his first patient?' and 'Sure it wasn't a vet?' and 'Never seen anything like it!'

He smiled at all the banter till he heard, 'You know this is going to hurt, don't you? Really hurt? Worse than you have been through?'

The driver looked at the nurse, not understanding what she meant. He didn't know that stitches were so painful to have taken out. He gulped and gave a sickly smile.

'Sit down there and hold on to the sides of the chair. Tell me when you are ready.'

Nonplussed, he sat down, gripped the seat and nodded, not sure if he was being fooled. There was a nurse either side of him, and they both gripped the Elastoplast near a jawbone. One yanked quickly up the right side of his face, and he yelped loudly; then, before it could register, the left one was yanked up. The ten-day-old beard felt as if it had been ripped out by the roots. His hands flew to his cheeks, holding them gently. His mouth dropped open, but, bravely, he didn't cry. He did swear under his breath, though. She'd been right.

The stitches weren't a problem—he didn't feel a thing. He had a small bald patch like an early monk, which in time grew over and that was that.

•

A week later, at the place where the truck had left the tarmac, Ron Phillips painted in huge, white letters that stretched from one side of the road to the other: 'RAY'S RETREAT ONE TREE'. He added a large white arrow pointing at the fallen tree. I bet Ron had a giggle painting that. The message was there for a long time, and so was the fallen tree. Nothing was ever discovered about who owned the cattle, so the boss had to wear the insurance costs. And you've probably guessed: the driver was yours truly.

The tree. It was one of the few large trees along that section of the road. A little bit the other way and the truck would have ended up in the farmer's paddock.

(To the memory of my rescuer and good friend Garry Freeman, who passed away in January 2009.)

11

Gypsies

In the late 1940s and early 1950s there were scruffy families that frequented the Melbourne road south of Sydney. We called them gypsies. They didn't have horses and caravans, though—oh no. They always had big, expensive American cars, reasonably late models, but always with that 'offish', grubby look about them: a dent here and there, with dirty, scuffed whitewall tyres. You could pick them a mile away.

I noticed one group quite often on the section of road between Camden and the highland town of Mittagong, usually about midday, give or take an hour or two. They had a large, black, late-model Buick with a Fisher Body (top of the range), only a couple of years old, and sure enough it would be on the side of the road with its bonnet up in the air. The doors would be open on the offside, with kids and adults sitting on the grass. There was always one male adult standing at the side, or at the front looking into the motor. Now, if you were innocent enough, you stopped to ask if they needed help. That's when the trap was set and a victim was caught. What pickings were there to be had? Sometimes it was just a gallon or two of fuel they succeeded in obtaining for nothing. (That's how they managed to operate such large cars—never buying fuel.)

Other times it went this way. The kind driver stopped in front of the Buick and a couple of the teenage girls rushed up to his windows on both sides. He was flooded with 'hellos', and then the girls asked, 'Can we bless your money?' They insisted the driver give them the money into their hands. If he did, he was lucky to get it all back. He was told to give them some so that the blessing would work. If he refused, they got up a noisy clamour to keep his attention. All the while this was going on, the adult was around the back of the victim's car siphoning petrol into a fuel can. One girl kept an eye on the siphoner and after a nod from him she dismissed the driver and walked away with the others, who then crowded around the man with the can of fuel so he couldn't be seen. The innocent, happy to be rid of them, drove off. It wasn't till the next time he needed fuel—thinking as he stopped that he was using more than usual—that he noticed his fuel cap was missing. (If he was a real innocent, before leaving the Buick he got out and looked into its motor with the adult male, who kept him busy, muttering, 'It stopped. Can you fix it?'

Meanwhile, the girls were up at his car, looking to see what was easy to steal.)

We truck drivers were annoyed by the gypsies' constant games of thieving from innocents. We would slow down and yell out, 'They're gypsies, mate. Watch out for your money and your petrol!' This always started the gang yelling, kids and all swearing at us to shut up and go away, accompanied by many rude hand gestures. We would just laugh, change down a gear and take off. What happened to the innocent after that was his concern; we had warned him.

The gypsies were around for a few years, many different groups with various cars, and then they just disappeared. I often wondered where they went.

12

Stubble trouble

In 1965 I was driving a Mack B61 with a McGrath wide-spread trailer for Mitchell Brothers. A load came up for Melbourne from Sydney, and as it was school holidays my son Ron, who was fourteen years old, asked if he could come for the ride. I was happy to say yes. It would give him an idea of what his old man did for a living—the long hours, the colourful people and the different places. It was getting on towards winter, and although the Mack had a reasonable heater we packed some warm clothes.

It was a fairly uneventful trip down the Hume Highway, and we reached Gundagai at about 8 pm for a meal break. As I was giving everything a check over out in the dark near the pumps, a youngish lady asked could I give her a lift to

Melbourne. She was all rugged up in an overcoat, wearing high heels, and she spoke okay, so I said yes but warned her it would be a bit cramped, as the Mack wasn't meant to carry more than a couple in the cab.

I did a final check, and we set off. The road was quite rough down past Kyeamba and through Little Billabong, and then onto the small town of Holbrook. There was a police station at Holbrook, but the local police didn't worry us much. It was always a good idea to just quietly saunter through the town and not make too much noise, though. You know what I mean: third gear, a gentle rumble, not too fast, then out into the darkness again and give it to her.

As the Mack idled down the main street I relaxed a little and looked across at young Ron, asleep against the door. As the streetlights flickered overhead I glanced at the young girl, who also had her head back, against the wall of the cabin. Something didn't seem right. *Hm*, I thought. *That's unusual— she wears a blonde wig.* The wig had moved out of kilter slightly and was too far over one ear. But then we were out of town, back into darkness, and there were other things to occupy my mind.

The run through to the Victorian border was easy. The town of Albury, on the New South Wales side, was spread out—a long few miles of houses and streetlights. As we trundled through the outskirts, my attention was drawn back to the lady passenger and her wig. That's when my eyes opened wide and I had to keep glancing quickly back and forth between her and the road ahead. I was puzzled at what I could see.

She had stubble showing through her make-up.

She must be a he, I thought. *Well, this is awkward.* I looked across at my young son, still sound asleep against the door. There is always that time in life when fathers have to have that important talk with their sons, but this didn't seem the moment to start explaining wigs and whiskers.

We went over the Murray River, the border between the two states, into Wodonga and Joe's Service Station, which was open all night, one of the few between Sydney and Melbourne. After fuelling I told the hitchhiker that I needed the whole seat now, for my son to sleep on, and I would have to leave 'her' there to catch another ride.

Without another word 'she' clip-clopped off to the all-night cafe. The Mack with my sleepy son and I disappeared into darkness once again. I breathed a sigh of relief that all was back to normal, then thought, *Come on, road, where's Melbourne?*

Ron Andrews

13

Ron Castell

Ron was a young Polish immigrant, about twenty-two years old, who worked on the dock at the factory where we loaded refrigerators for delivery interstate. He had come from Europe on an assisted passage, total cost to him £10. He was what we called a New Australian in those days.

He was always pestering us for a job driving one of the trucks. Our usual answer? 'See the boss.' Sometimes, when the boss came to the dock to give the driver money for his trip, Ron would waylay him, selling himself as a terrific driver. The boss was fairly casual about such requests and would tell Ron he would think about it if a job came up. This went on for about a year, till all of a sudden one day in 1954 the boss came to the dock and, before Ron could corner him, beckoned him over and asked, 'Have you got a driving licence?'

'Of course,' said Ron. He took his wallet out and showed the boss his pride and joy—his New South Wales drivers licence. 'Was best driver in all Poland. Am good driver,' he said.

Back in those medieval times, the late 1940s and 1950s, a drivers licence allowed you to drive anything but a green plate truck, a motorbike and a bus. A green plate truck needed a driver with a green plate licence, because that type of truck was allowed to be hired like a taxi to carry goods, with the driver paid in cash. To have a green plate licence was the best—you were tops. No criminal record and a clean drivers licence were just the first requirements.

The boss looked briefly at Ron's standard drivers licence, nodded and said, 'My driver Dave is sick, and the truck has to leave tonight for Melbourne. Do you think you could get it there?'

'Of course,' said Ron. Then he asked, 'Which way is Melbourne? Over Harbour Bridge or the other way?'

The boss did a double take and said, hesitatingly, after a pause, 'The other way.'

'That's good. I know that road very well. Have been to Liverpool many times, a long way.'

Liverpool is an outer suburb of Sydney on the Melbourne highway, only 25 miles from the centre of Sydney, while Melbourne was another 550 miles, up and down steep mountain ranges, along dangerous narrow roads, round blind curves and over untold numbers of single-lane bridges. Still, of all the road trips, Sydney to Melbourne was called the Schoolboy Run: it was sealed all the way and the least dangerous.

The boss's brain was clicking faster than a computer as he looked at Ron. There was not one single other driver available—he had been looking all morning. He sighed and said to Ron, 'I'll get you a road map.'

'Ah, that is good. Now I cannot go wrong way.'

The boss decided that Ron couldn't get into too much trouble. It was only a light load of refrigerators, not over-loaded. He'd be there in a couple of days and could backload from Melbourne a couple of Standard Vanguard cars. Then Dave could take over and, all going well, Ron could drive the little flat-top truck around town.

Dave's truck was an Albion Clydesdale four-cylinder diesel motor fitted with vacuum brakes. The air breather for the motor was attached to the top of the engine cover inside the cabin, next to the driver. Because it was a forward-control cabin with the motor beside the driver it made a hell of a noise all the time, sucking air into the motor, and it was worse when it was going down a mountain using its vacuum-brake system—nearly as noisy as the exhaust brakes of today's monsters, except this noise was inside the cabin. No wonder all the old truckies from that era are deaf. This wonderful monstrosity was coupled to a 30-foot trailer, also with vacuum brakes, which had to be operated separately by a lever under the steering wheel and were good for about three or four applications before they overheated and were

Albion Clydesdale, early 1950s.

useless. The top speed on a flat road was 28 miles per hour. That was the governed speed; there was no rev counter. The instruments consisted of a speedometer, amp meter, voltage regulator and vacuum gauge—that was it.

A tiny windscreen wiper was attached to the top of the windscreen and driven by a small electric motor. This took great delight, when it was windy and raining, in being bullied into sweeping off the windscreen and up into the night sky to play cricket back and forth with the raindrops in the dark, ignoring the explosive abuse of the alarmed driver as he frantically yanked his side window down and tried to peer through the rain and still stay on the road, juggling steering wheel, trailer brakes, foot brake and gears. Sounds easy, doesn't it? It wasn't—it was instant, icy-cold panic—but without thinking the driver would do everything needed to keep it all under control. The wiper in the sky seemed to always happen when running out of brakes down a steep and dangerous road on a mountain somewhere.

Ron was given a trial run around the block at Dave's house. The Albion was slow but strong, and as long as the driver could master the art of changing gear up or down by double-declutching then it was very forgiving. Ron muddled through and was given the permit that allowed him to legally carry goods to the Victorian border, 350 miles away, and money to pay for the other permit needed to cross Victoria to Melbourne. With his road map open at the Sydney-to-Yass section, off he went, with the Albion belching smoke, one or two gear crunches and the boss wondering, *Have I done the right thing?*

•

Well, our firm was the joke of the road for quite a while after Ron's first trip. No matter where we pulled up at a cafe or service station some truck driver would yell out, 'Where's your road map? You can borrow mine; I don't need one. Are you looking for Brisbane or Melbourne? It's a long way, mate. Don't get lost—take my map.' It seemed that on that trip Ron stopped every truck coming down the road towards him, waving his Golden Fleece road map at the driver and asking, 'This road to Melbourne—yes?' On being told it was, he would then ask, 'How far? Many miles yet?' Again told it was he would shake his head and, looking at the map with his finger pointing roughly to where he thought he was, he would mutter, 'So far away yet. Must be I get there soon. Thank you, thank you for help. I go now.' Then he would point down the road and run back to his truck, which was waiting patiently.

He made Melbourne okay, found the delivery address, loaded two cars and trundled back to Sydney by following the towns he had circled with pen on the prized map. It was his most valuable possession till he had been to all the capital cities. 'Australia is bigger than Europe and much more danger for truck driver, but for me no problem,' he said to the boss on his return, before asking, 'How much you pay? Where I go next?'

Ron put in many years of hard slog with those slow Clydesdales. He was very reliable and honest, and always tried to please. Nothing was a problem that he couldn't fix, except for one time not long after he started to drive for the boss. He had become a little too assured and overconfident of his ability, as was sometimes a problem back in those early, dangerous days. Taking chances with machines that were out of their depth in this country, unable to offer even a reasonable amount of safety to the poor driver, was an everyday hazard.

At this time, around 1955, the number one highway in Australia, the Sydney-to-Melbourne Hume Highway, was only a dual-carriage road sealed all the way apart from some odd patches that local councils were slow to keep up to scratch. It wasn't the superhighway of today, bypassing towns and sweeping through the countryside avoiding steep and winding climbs up and down the mountains. Back then there were single-lane bridges and sharp curves that leant the wrong way. The road just followed the original bullock tracks joining country towns, and if you continued from town to town in the general direction of the desired capital city you would eventually arrive at your destination.

One thing that hadn't even been thought of then was a lane in the centre of the road for vehicles waiting to turn right. And that was Ron's undoing. He had a full load of refrigerators from the factory in Sydney where he had once been a dock hand, destination Melbourne. After leaving Sydney the night before the delivery was due he stopped for a sleep, lying over the engine in the cabin for a couple of hours. Later, he left Gundagai behind and climbed up Sylvias, a steep hill that needed a low gear up to the cutting at the top. Down the other side was a steep decline, and at the bottom was the turn-off to the town of Wagga Wagga, on the right-hand side of and at a right angle to the highway.

If you were a stranger wanting Wagga Wagga you would stop and check the little road sign at the intersection. We old-timers of the road were careful going down to the Wagga turn-off. If the road was clear of traffic you could let the truck run up to governed speed and then throw it into neutral and coast down, reaching the speed of sound, like a space rocket, being able to see the road all the way up the valley and knowing that the old girl would eventually bleed off speed and could be flicked back into top gear without the use of the clutch, so making up a bit of time. But if a car overtook you on the way up the climb you had to go very slowly down the other side in case the car's driver decided to stop in the middle of the road and check the signpost to Wagga. He might only hesitate, he might turn right, and then again he might just barrel on down the road. It wasn't till he was committed that we knew what we had to do. But Ron hadn't encountered any cars at the Wagga turn-off in the few trips he had completed, so there was a disaster just waiting to happen.

Now, what happened wasn't really all Ron's fault. He chugged up the Sylvias side and started down the other when a little Austin A40 sedan overtook him. He had enough sense to pull the trailer brakes on a little so he wasn't speeding, and then, lo and behold, the Austin, which was a way ahead, came to a stop to read the sign. To compound the problem, a couple of cars were coming the opposite way, from Tarcutta, taking up the other side of the road. Ron slammed the trailer brakes full on and trod hard on the foot brake, blowing the horn and seeing himself shunting the little Austin all the way to Albury, 90 miles further on, with one whack.

The signpost was on the edge of the road, and behind it was a flimsy wire fence keeping a dozen or so cattle in their nice grassy paddock, with only a couple of large trees in it. There was either going to be a dreadful car smash on the Wagga turn-off, or Ron could take her into the paddock and maybe kill a cow. That's what he did. He yanked the wheel, just missed the back of the Austin, annihilated the signpost and tore the fence out, sending wooden posts like boomerangs into the air.

The poor old Clydesdale was still going at about 25 miles per hour, with Ron bouncing up and down, hitting the steel roof with his head, his legs banging on the underside of the steering wheel, trying to steer but not having much luck, dust and dirt filling the cabin. In that paddock there was one large old stump of a tree nearly as wide as the truck's cabin, and, you guessed it, he hit that stump smack in the centre of his radiator. The trailer broke the turntable and slid up to the back of the cabin, but luckily by then it was at about walking speed and just stopped.

Ron couldn't see—his eyes were full of dust—and the pain from his legs was so severe he thought he had broken them both above the knee. And his head hurt. The Austin wandered off down the road, not wanting to go to Wagga Wagga anyway.

The driver's door wouldn't open, so Ron crawled out of the window and lowered himself to the ground, looking towards the highway, shaking his fist and shouting in Polish where he wanted to shove that little Austin sedan. But the object of his rage seemed to be unaware of anything going on around him and slowly disappeared out of sight at the end of the valley.

Some people in other cars arrived at the scene having witnessed at least part of what had happened, and they ran over to see if Ron was okay. It turned out that he had slight concussion and very bruised legs, but nothing broken. He was given a lift into Tarcutta, the next town on the way to Melbourne, only about 6 miles further on.

According to the story we heard, Ron told the boss that if he could get the turntable back in position and a tow back to the road he might be only a day late into Melbourne. It was arranged that the local tow-truck man would take Ron back out and check the damage, then report to the boss.

The report given to the boss was as follows. On coming to a stop at the tree trunk, the radiator had buried itself into the fan. Both fan and radiator needed replacing. The force on stopping had broken the tail shaft at the rear universal joint. The front engine mounts were broken, as well as the rear gearbox mount. The cabin was buckled and neither door would open. The turntable was adrift and buckled. All the U-bolts were severed, the drive axle had been forced back, all the spring hangers were broken, and the differential pinion was suspect due to the broken tail shaft.

When this was all pointed out to Ron, he told the tow-truck driver that the load looked okay and asked him to tell the boss to send an empty truck and he would tranship the load. Maybe he would then be only a couple of days late into Melbourne.

The next day an empty truck arrived, but when the load was uncovered they saw that the handle of every refrigerator had broken and was jammed into the back of the next refrigerator. (They were not in crates; there was only a canvas cover over each refrigerator.) Every one had to be sent back to the Sydney factory and repaired. The Albion Clydesdale was towed to Sydney and written off.

*

I did my time in Clydesdales as well. They were tough, slow, reliable, but bloody dangerous. We made them do the impossible. I bet if the truck manufacturers in Britain who designed those vehicles based on 1930s standards for their little island and for maybe half-day trips could see what we in our huge continent did with them in the 1950s, always in danger, every trip a new adventure, they would shake their heads in wonder.

Across the Nullarbor Plain to Perth: twelve days, maybe more, temperature so hot the gear lever burnt a scar on the left leg, or the radiator overheating and covering the driver with scalding-hot water through the open windscreen. A tiny seat, with practically no padding. Always, the never-ending choking, sucking roar of the air intake inside the cabin next to the steering wheel. Slipping and sliding in the snow and ice on top of Black Mountain. Overrunning the governors near the bottom of the lower Moonbi Range and throwing it into 'angel gear', hoping like hell you can have all the road for the next 5 miles to the township of Kootingal to bring it under control. The speed bleeding off slowly, allowing you to click it back into gear, bathed in cold sweat and hair standing on end, fiercely determined not to be beaten, and, after the danger slips back into its black box, thinking, *What am I doing here?*

Sometimes, on such occasions, to let off steam I would scream and yell into the dark night, 'Bastards! You're all bastards!' I'm not sure who I was yelling at. The boss, for not paying a better wage? The truck manufacturers, for making these antiquated trucks that belonged back in the 1930s, before the Second World War? Or the transport inspectors in their web, waiting like spiders to pounce? The police safety bureau on their motorbikes, hiding at cemetery gates? Bored police waiting on country roads to book you for doing a couple of miles per hour over the speed limit while 100 miles out in the bush? Bored inspectors waiting on main roads, another set of spiders, hoping you were overloaded even just a little? I guess I was yelling at all of them in a way, but I always felt better afterwards and had a gulp of flat lemonade, lit a cigarette, talked to the old girl about us against them. Just a little bit drained of energy but ready for the next round of trouble, saying softly, 'You won't beat me,' and drumming my fingers on the steering wheel, smiling slightly and concentrating on the road ahead.

14

Just a phone call away

The Nullarbor Plain is a place of extremes: hot or cold, wet or dry. When it rained, in places the track became a canal of water, or a slippery, sliding ribbon of mud. There was no room for error, and a driver worked harder than any rally-car driver just to keep going and stay on the track, hoping every long puddle of water didn't hide a wombat hole.

In 1958 I was lumbering along in second and third gears in a Foden prime mover, pulling a 1500-cubic-foot Pantech with a full load of furniture. It had rained a few days earlier, turning the road into a driver's nightmare, slipping and sliding. It was trying to push me off the track, left or right, depending on which way it was sliding at the time. *Oops, there she goes again* . . . I'd correct quickly, hoping like hell I was in time to stop her sinking into the soft edges.

I had been doing well. I'd left the Nullarbor Station home-stead some time back and was hoping to make Koonalda Station before perhaps waiting a day for the road to dry a little more. I knew I would be welcome there, as I was the unofficial postman and delivery man for the few hardy souls who made the plain their home. Scobie Beatty at Nullarbor Station had advised Cyril Gurney at Koonalda Station that I should arrive sometime late that day. I was looking forward to relaxing with a beer or two with Cyril.

That's when it happened. I bounced out of two big ruts in the road, and then she careened to the right, as if I were on a greasy plank, down into the muddy bog between the road and the surrounding bush. I gave her a try in low gear, not liking my chances, but she wouldn't move. If anything she settled further down into the mud. *Nuh, no go. Switch the motor off.*

I looked out of my side window, and if I had opened the driver's door I would have tumbled straight into the mud, the whole rig—prime mover and huge van—was leaning at such a steep angle. I froze for a moment, not game to move. Then started the *What do I do?* thinking. *I know! I'll ring Nullarbor Station, and maybe Koonalda, who are expecting me, and see if they can help in any way. They are just a phone call away.*

I gingerly let the driver's door swing open and leapt out and over the mud to a dry patch. After surveying the lean and how deep the wheels were in the mud, I knew I needed help. I had to make that phone call.

This abrupt stop of mine took place approximately halfway between the two stations, and quite a distance from both; in fact, I was not far east of the Western Australian border. Now, when situations like this overtook us, we overlanders, as we were called, would shake our heads and wonder why we went out there looking for trouble. And how was I going to make a phone call out in the sticks, hundreds of miles from anybody? There were no public phone boxes out on the plain.

But I had an ace up my sleeve: I carried a phone with me. I'm not pulling your leg—I had a working portable telephone. And not a mobile telephone. This was fifty years before mobiles had even been thought of. I had an ex-army crank-type telephone that I kept wrapped up in the cabin. With a bit of ingenuity I had learnt how to make a long-distance call or yell for help out there if needed, and this was definitely a yell-for-help time.

Set mostly beside the road was the one and only telegraph line, going east to west—just one sagging line, between wooden poles that stood at all angles, connecting the stations. Primitive, defying the elements, it was the only link to the outside world. I had learnt to throw the line from my army phone up and over the telegraph line, and to earth it by peeing into a scooped-out hole beside the pole and jamming the end of the earth wire into the piddly mud. Then I could talk to the nearest station for free—although everyone else connected to the outback system could listen in. On some trips I would crank it up and have a cheap chat to Melbourne or Perth, linked courtesy of the nearest station, for whom the cost was only about 3 cents a call. Those were the days, Telstra! Actually, it was called the PMG in those days: the

Postmaster-General's Department. They handled letters, telephones and telegrams.

Anyway, I cranked three long and two short rings—the number for Nullarbor Station—and, hey presto, I was through. 'Hey, Scobie, it's Barrie. I'm bogged about halfway between you and Cyril.'

'No problem,' he said, 'we'll be on the way with some old railway sleepers and tools as soon as possible.'

Cyril at Koonalda, who had listened in, piped up and said they were on their way as well.

A few hours later they trickled in from east and west. In the meantime I had been digging away at the wheels, ready to try to put planks under them. We dug long ditches around the wheels and drained the water away, then laid the sleepers down and, with a bit of luck and with me having a little talk to 'her' at the same time, out she came, none the worse, back up on the greasy centre of the road. After all that, it was decided that a barbecue was in order.

Barrie Sculley

15

The Tea and Sugar train

In the late 1950s we early pioneers of the overland trail across the Nullarbor Plain were offered a new way to cross the desert. The Trans-Australian Railway would transport our trucks from Port Augusta to Kalgoorlie. It was very expensive, but it saved weeks of tough driving and wear and tear on the truck and driver. There were two systems operating. The first was the crack passenger train with silver service and private compartments. It was one of the top ten trains in the world at that time. The second was the goods train, which slowly wended its way across the desert, stopping at every fettlers' camp that needed supplies. It was called the Tea and Sugar train. That was the train we were allowed to use. Some flat-top railcars were added to the train, and we drove up an earthen bank and carefully and slowly trundled from flat car to flat car over small reinforced plates to the allocated railcar. The railway staff chained the trucks down, and we then had to go to the rear of the train, carrying our bedding and enough food to last the journey. A daytime departure was not so bad, but if it was leaving at night it was damned difficult to stumble over rail lines in a dark goods yard that covered acres of land, carrying everything needed for a long train trip.

The cost in today's values was about $2000 for the truck, and we had to pay a single fare for the privilege of cooking our own meals and finding somewhere to sleep. Attached to the rear of the train were a couple of old-style coaches with wooden seats and benches where we drivers could lie down. (That was if there were no relief staff or railway personnel who needed them; if that was the case, then we slept on the floor.) For our meals we were allowed to cook on the primitive wood stove in the rear guard's van after any rail staff were finished using it.

One time, crossing to Perth on the Tea and Sugar train, we were held up on a loop line waiting for the passenger train to come through. It always had right of way. There were four of us that trip with trucks loaded up front on the flat cars behind the locomotives, including Bob Taylor, a short, plump bloke who drove a Leyland. We were housed half a mile away from our trucks, next to the guard's van way down at the rear of the train.

It seemed that the passenger train was running late and we were to be held up for an hour at least. It was early afternoon, and Bob could see some tents and a Blitz wagon parked a little way off so decided to climb down from the train and go over to have a look and a yarn. The other drivers and I were content just to sit as still as possible in the shade; we were sweating enough, as it was over 100 degrees in the sun.

Time crawled past, but eventually we could see the passenger train coming so knew we would be on the way again soon. The guard, who had been yarning with us, suddenly realised Bob was still missing. This spot in the desert was no place to be left behind.

We started to yell loudly to him, waving our arms. 'Hey, Bob! Bob! Quick, it's time to go. Hurry up, ya stupid bastard!' There was flurry over at the camp site, and darn me if Bob couldn't be seen bowling two huge 1000 × 20 tyres over towards us as we stood in the doorway of the guard's van.

'What the hell is he doing?' one of the drivers exclaimed.

'Looks like he has a couple of tyres,' said someone else.

With a lot of concentration and a few mishaps, with a tyre now and then falling over and a scramble to get it upright again, Bob managed to get the tyres to the bottom of the siding, near the open sliding door of the guard's van. He stood down there looking up at us, about 10 feet below the door, holding on to one tyre, with the other plopped over flat on the ground. 'Quick, give us a hand—I just bought 'em,' he said.

With a bit of prompting, two of the boys jumped down and grabbed one of the tyres, then manhandled it up the embankment to the rail line below the door, and two of us

The Tea and Sugar train.

reached down, and with them lifting and us pulling up she came into the van.

We heard a train whistle, and just then the passenger train roared past on the other side. A quick heave and yank, and the second tyre was up on the guard's van floor. Then we reached down and helped the three men up just in time, as the train had started to roll.

The guard wasn't happy about the tyres, as they took up too much floor space in his cramped van, and he ordered Bob to get rid of them and didn't care where. Between us we bowled them from the van across the swaying couplings to the little carriage next along, where we were housed. The only place they would fit was in the corridor, and for the rest of the journey they banged back and forth, up and down it. They were too wide to lie flat. We asked Bob why he had bought them, and he said they had been out there for years, never used, so he'd bought them cheap.

An afternoon and a night later we arrived at Parkeston, the rail yard for the gold-mining town of Kalgoorlie, where we drove the trucks off the train with only 400 miles of sealed road to drive to Perth. None of us were happy about helping Bob get his two new tyres along the many rail lines to his truck, but we did, complaining all the time.

A few days later some of us were in the Sharfston Hotel, which was our watering hole while we waited for something to load back east, and Bob breezed in looking for a beer.

'Put the new tyres on yet?' I asked him.

'Um, not yet,' said Bob. 'And you know what? I could've bought them two tyres cheaper here in Perth than what I paid for them out bloody there.'

'Well, ya know what, old son? They're about to cost ya more, as it's your shout for the rest of the night.'

16

The Lame Duck

He was young and wanted to get into the new adventure of long-distance road transport in Australia. It was 1956 and big things were happening. The old tax had been abolished, and it was possible to make a living now—still tough, but better than it had been before. He worked on the dispatch dock where the freight was loaded onto those big monsters with fourteen wheels; with the tarpaulins tied down they disappeared up the street not to be seen or heard of till they parked outside the delivery address in some faraway city, days or even weeks later. That's what he wanted to do: drive one of those monsters.

He grabbed all the overtime he could and saved all his money. But those big trucks were bloody expensive. Not many around second-hand; a new one was out of the question. Every Saturday he would scan the papers till finally one day he saw a truck and single-axle trailer for sale, the price around what he could afford. Sure, it was a European make, not many around, but the nearest thing he had seen that was in reach of his bank account. The asking price was a little bit more than he could afford, but he had an idea. His mate Ron had said he would buy his Austin A40 at a fair price if he needed extra cash. So he knew he was around the mark.

The address was the other side of Parramatta, quite a way from where he lived. He rattled his way out there in the Austin; the owner of the truck had said he would be home all day. He was pleasantly surprised when he saw the truck—it looked fairly clean, tyres were about fifty per cent and the motor sounded okay. After a test drive around the block with the owner showing him that it changed gear okay, it was a done deal.

He said he would be back on Monday with the cash. No, he didn't have a deposit. The owner shrugged his shoulders, hoping he had made a sale. So far it was the only offer and he was anxious to get rid of it.

Ron agreed to buy the car but wouldn't have the money till later in the week. Okay, that money would help cover his operating expenses till some earnings started rolling in.

Monday came. He went to the bank, withdrew his money, leaving enough with the car money from Ron to operate the truck for a couple of weeks. He arrived at the seller's house and emptied his pockets of all the cash onto the kitchen table. It was about £500 short, but the seller couldn't grab the money quickly enough. He hadn't had another viewer for his truck and he so desperately wanted to sell it. So he signed the papers, and our young truck driver jumped in the cabin and took off, not crunching too many gears, thinking he was in seventh heaven.

At home he rolled out the tarpaulins—two large ones and a long cap tarp that stretched from the front of the load to the rear. A few patches, but in general good condition. He checked the motor, gearbox, differential and tail shaft. Everything seemed okay. After washing it he stood back and admired his key to the future.

●

He loaded his first trip: the easy road, to Melbourne. He had a full load of Malleys kerosene 'Warmas'. They were bulky but light. The tarps covered them well. He filled the tanks with diesel, bought a bottle of lemonade and a packet of boiled lollies for him, and he was off on his first great adventure.

He reached the town of Yass that first day with no trouble. The second day was a bit different. Australia is the driest land in the world, and the summer heat is quite fierce. It takes its toll on drivers and trucks. About an hour out of Yass he glanced down at the instruments and saw the temperature needle climbing quickly, too quickly. He pulled over onto the grass on the side of the road with a frown. He could smell heat.

The top radiator hose was on its last days; steam was puffing out of a small crack near the clamp. Luckily, there was enough to slice that section off and reclamp the pipe, which he did, then set off again, not too concerned. He made it to the little garage at Colac and replaced the hose with a universal type, as the garage didn't keep parts for his make of truck. In fact, as time went on he found it difficult to buy anything anywhere on the road for his truck, always having to make do as best he could. And he needed parts quite often over the next couple of years. It was a comfortable truck to drive—soft ride, heater in winter, good seat adjustment—but the bloody thing kept breaking down. Mostly it was little things, like copper fuel lines would crack; the electrics had a habit of blowing fuses for no reason; filters would clog up, even new ones; and injector pipes would split. The only place he could buy parts for it was in the capital city where he'd bought it. So he carried a toolbox full of spares.

So many times he stood beside the road in oil-stained shorts and shirt, with a spanner in his hand, grease up to his elbows, or rolled under the truck muttering to himself about his own stupidity in buying this heap of 'nuts and bolts.' He would make a face, thinking of the dispatch manager warning him not to be late again this time, which he was, usually, and looking with envy at the trucks swishing past while he tried to fix another problem on his 'lame duck'. That's what he named her—the Lame Duck—painted on the front bumper bar.

One day in the early summer of his second year, while in Melbourne waiting for a back load to Sydney, he was offered a run to Perth. He laughed. He had enough trouble running Sydney to Melbourne. In fact, he'd only taken one load to Brisbane in all that time, as it was such a tough run—600 miles to the north, up and down the New England High Country.

Perth was 3000 miles away from Melbourne across a desert of over 1000 miles where the road was a dirt track. Having a drink or two with some other drivers that night in the pub he mentioned the Perth trip. After much talk and many beers he was convinced he could do it, that Perth run. Why not? It was good money, and the best part was that if he could get a full load back, which was hard to do, it would make the trip a huge success money-wise. At the end of the drinking session he could see himself back from Perth, taking delivery of a new International 180, his small bank account swollen with the Perth money plus the Lame Duck as a full deposit. *Yes*, he said to himself as he wobbled to his feet, leaning on the bar, *I can do it. I can. Perth, here I come.*

Grog and good ideas don't often go together. The trip across was like nothing the driver could ever have imagined. It was so hot and dry, like a furnace, during the day. Then the nights were as cold as a freezing-cold winter's night in the High Country. The days dragged on—bits falling off, water hoses splitting, pipes cracking, stopping, repairing, starting, stopping—that track called a road could shake your teeth loose.

He decided to drive at night—not so hot—but the lights blew and he had no spare bulbs. So he went back to day travel, drenched in sweat, constantly wiping his face with a towel, calling himself all the names he could think of for being such an idiot and even thinking of tackling this bloody desert. He talked to the Lame Duck all the time, encouragingly some-times, but more and more angrily as the days passed.

But he finally made it to Perth. He couldn't believe he had actually got there. He unloaded, got drunk for a day and wondered how the hell he was going to get back east over that bloody awful track.

He did the rounds for a back load without much luck. A few people said, 'Maybe next week.' His timing was bad, because just that week Ansett Transport was advertising around the streets of Perth with a large, colourful banner on a truck to send goods with them, as they had a contract to piggyback trucks across the wilderness from the east on the Trans-Australian Railway. No dust, no breakdowns, goods always on time. Bloody hell, what next?

After ten days it was clear there was no loading east for him. So much for the new truck, and, worse, the empty drive back to the east. Damn.

•

Now, Peter, a driver for another firm, had watched the Lame Duck having its innards tampered with on the side of the road on nearly every trip over the previous two years. He had helped now and then, feeling sorry for the young driver. Peter was driving west over the Nullarbor Plain to Perth one early summer day. It was hot, damn hot, and the dust was drifting over the cab—like being in a vacuum cleaner. The track was so rough that he had been in second gear all morning and couldn't outrun the dust. But he was used to it: he'd been doing the run for a while, and the money was good.

In the late afternoon, the dust cleared for a bit, and he thought he could see smoke on the horizon. Now, that was a worry. The low scrub in sections sometimes caught alight from the odd lightning strike or even from the sun on a broken bottle, and that could be big trouble. A fire could have a mile-wide front, with nowhere for a truck to escape. It was nearly impossible to turn around, and if the wind increased, the fire would overtake a slow truck anyway.

Peter squinted into the sun with all these thoughts racing through his head, hoping like hell it was just someone's camp fire. After a couple of minutes, he could see it wasn't a scrub fire, thank goodness. It was not wide enough, and was coming only from one spot on or near the road ahead. Rattling up closer he could see it was a truck on fire, smoke billowing under and around it, and a figure appeared to be jumping in and out of the smoke, probably trying to put it out with sand from the track. Poor bastard.

A Leyland Beaver truck had caught fire a year before 300 miles back along the road; its remains were still there. It had been carrying a load of gas bottles: oxygen and acetylene. Something had happened—no one knew what—but it had caught fire and the bottles apparently went off like torpedoes all over the place.

Peter pulled up about two trailer lengths away, just to be safe, then with his fire extinguisher ran into the thick smoke towards the burning truck. A figure loomed out of the smoke, running hard away from the truck. Peter hesitated, thinking the fuel tanks were going to blow up. Then he recognised the figure: it was the young driver he had seen so many times on the side of the road the last couple of years. 'I've only got a small extinguisher. Where's the worst bit?' he yelled, the smoke starting to make him cough and bring tears to his eyes.

'Throw that bloody thing away and get more wood, mate. I'm burning the bastard!' the driver replied, running to get broken bits of wood that were lying around the edge of the road. He wasn't helping matters any.

Fuel had been leaking all over the exhaust system for some time, and even as far back as the empty trailer, it seemed, and something had set it off—heat, cigarette butt, who knows?— and when it had burst into flames it was too late anyway.

•

Peter saw the driver about three months later, driving a brand-new red International 180 with a fully loaded 32-foot trailer out of Melbourne. He gave Peter a thumbs up, with a grin from ear to ear, as he passed. Painted on the front bumper bar in large, stylish letters was 'Flying High'.

17

A moving trunk

The telephone rang from its hiding place among all the papers, invoices and usual mess that seem to cover a busy manager's desk. Jock Paling picked up the receiver. 'Hullo, Mercury Transport,' he said, cradling it on his right shoulder while both hands proceeded to file some invoices into a large envelope.

'This is Taronga Park Zoo,' a metallic voice replied.

Jock raised his eyes to the ceiling, immediately flipping through voices in his head of drivers who, maybe, were trying to pull a fast one on him. The favourite prank was 'Is that the Chinese laundry?' He dismissed all the known pranksters and was left with a blank. At the same time he was wondering why, if the caller was for real, Taronga Park Zoo would call an interstate trucking company. 'This is Mercury Transport,' Jock repeated. 'How can I help you?'

The driver, Mick Stephens (far left) looks on as elephant keeper Dave stands on the spare wheel, talking to the elephant. The load also consisted of a few President refrigerators (at the rear) and the elephant's meals (the bales at the front). Can you see the trunk?

The voice answered, 'As you know, Sir Edward Hallstrom of Hallstroms refrigerators has a very keen input into Taronga Park Zoo. He has suggested we ring you as your firm has an excellent record of delivering refrigerators long distances without being crated. In other words, having a good track record handling delicate goods.'

'Thank you for the compliment, but we don't handle Hallstroms refrigerators.'

'This is not about refrigerators.'

'Oh, I see,' said Jock. 'What's it about?'

'An elephant.'

Jock's brain was going at 1000 miles an hour. It was not a driver's voice, but that didn't mean a driver hadn't put someone up to the prank. 'Listen, whoever you are, I'm busy and do not have the time for crank calls,' he said, and hung up. He went back to his sorting.

The phone immediately rang again.

'Hullo, Mercury Transport.'

'Please don't hang up; this *is* Taronga Park Zoo calling. We have to deliver an elephant to Adelaide Zoo, and Sir Edward Hallstrom recommended we ring you people to see how feasible it would be to truck it across. I know it must sound like a joke, but it isn't. Believe me. We are looking for ideas how to do it.'

'What's your name and number? I'll ring you back,' said Jock, still not sure of the call.

After some time on the phone it was established that, yes, there was an elephant, not a fully grown elephant but not a baby either, that had to be delivered to Adelaide Zoo. It weighed a few tons and stood about 10 feet tall.

Reg Phillips had in his fleet of trucks a fairly new International 160 with a 32-foot single-axle trailer that could carry freight heavier than this elephant, so that was the one to use. It was agreed that it could be done with a large open-top crate built onto the rigid-tray truck for extra strength, with a tarpaulin over the top but not quite covering the whole of the crate so that air and sunlight could reach the elephant's head.

The sides of the crate would reach the elephant's shoulders, allowing it to see out and around. The head keeper from the zoo would go with the elephant all the way, as he knew how to control it.

•

Dave the keeper and Mick the driver had quite an adventurous trip to Adelaide, with a lot of laughs. At one point they pulled in to Mittagong, where transport inspectors always waited to check where trucks were going, what was on board and the weight of the consignment. First Mick was asked how heavy the load was, and he said, with a straight face, 'Depends how many legs are on the floor at the same time and how much crap we've shovelled off. It varies all the time.'

'Don't be smart,' said the inspector. 'What type of freight are you carrying?'

'Animal,' said Mick. 'Oh, and some refrigerators.'

'What do you mean, animal?'

'An elephant,' Mick replied, poker-faced.

That didn't go over big at all. The inspector looked angrily up at Mick in the cabin, grunted, and moved down towards the tray of the truck. He grabbed the gate side and heaved himself up onto the truck, balancing himself on the combing and raising his arm to reach for the top of the crate.

At that moment, for no reason, the elephant roared and swung his trunk high in the air and then groped with it down over the side, sniffing near the inspector's head. With a cry of terror the inspector dropped his clipboard, fell back down onto the road, scrambled upright and took off across the highway at 1000 miles an hour. Halfway across, he stopped and looked back. His face had turned a grey colour; his mouth was open and his eyes were wide. He could not believe what had happened. In the meantime the elephant had withdrawn its trunk, and nothing of it could be seen—just a big crate with a tarp over part of it. The truck rocked a little as the elephant shuffled around inside.

By this time Mick and Dave had walked around to the same side of the truck and nearly pissed themselves with laughter, watching the inspector running off across the road. The inspector's mate came around the front of the truck, and he was grinning as well. Nonplussed by the prospect of cataloguing Mick, his animal and a genuine elephant keeper, the inspectors decided it was beyond anything they had answers for, so Mick, Dave and the elephant were waved on without further ado.

Their progress through the country towns en route to Adelaide caused quite a stir whenever a roar and a wave of the trunk coincided with a stop. The elephant preferred the wind to be on it and always complained when they stopped, but after a few minutes settled down.

All ended well, and we had reports over the years that the elephant was thriving and enjoying its new home.

18

A comet came to Earth

In the mid 1950s I worked for McNealy and Debney. They had a contract with Goodyear Tyres for delivery of new tyres to Melbourne from the Sydney factory. Old McNealy was cunning: he would send a new driver off from Sydney on the run to Melbourne, wait twenty or thirty minutes and then follow him in his car. He knew how long it should take the driver to get to Razorback Mountain, outside Sydney, allowing for the traffic at that time of day or night, and he expected to catch up with him before the mountain, all things being equal. If he caught up with the truck before or at the bottom of the mountain, it showed that the driver was steady, and that was acceptable. If he had to climb the mountain to catch the truck, it meant the driver was maybe a little fast, which could be a problem, as a load of tyres was very unstable. McNealy would remind the driver to be extra careful and to take it steady. He would hand the driver some paperwork that had been left behind, so all looked okay.

I took one of the International 180s on my first trip, and when McNealy caught up with me I was exactly where he had hoped to find me, at the bottom of the mountain. Because I had years of experience on diesel trucks by that time, a few months later, when the Leyland driver left, I was given the Leyland, as most of the drivers were not familiar with it. They were only experienced with petrol motors, not with a motor that had a governor fitted and no two-speed button on the gear lever.

●

It happened on a lonely stretch of road about 50 miles north of the town of Albury, on the way to Melbourne. I was roughly on time, nearing the Victorian border at about midday, cruising along, and coming up to a bend in the road, not very sharp, just a gentle correction of the steering wheel needed. I noticed this car coming towards me, travelling very fast, and seeming to take up too much of the road. In fact, as we approached each other my heart started to race: he was heading straight for me, on my side of the road, making no attempt to take the bend. I quickly moved over a little, but he kept coming across, further and further, heading straight for my driver's door.

I moved even further towards the edge, kicking up the dirt

on the side of the road, but he continued coming straight for me, and, worse, the road at this point was raised a little. Tyres made a high load inclined to bounce around, not very stable. Within seconds it was time either to go off the road, down the bank, to try to dodge him, or to attempt to take the bend, to stay on the road, which was the automatic choice. It was at that second that the car swerved sharply and shot past me with about 12 inches to spare between us. How he missed the back trailer wheels beat me, but he did, and he kept going.

Had the driver fallen asleep, or what? But that was the least of my worries. The high edge of the road was crumbling away beneath me as I tried to turn into the bend gradually and stay on the road, hoping everything would keep upright. But I was just too far over: the drive wheels were digging in and slipping down the embankment. The whole load of tyres started to lean. I could feel her going. The adrenalin was pumping, and my eyes were probably as big as saucers. I didn't have time to panic, just held on, and then there was a huge bang, the trailer turntable pin let go, and the trailer came free and tipped over on its side, skidding to a halt in the grass off the road like a Wild West covered wagon chased by Indians.

This caused the prime mover—with me holding on like grim death—to half flip up in the air and down again onto her wheels, and then to fishtail a little. The one and only gum tree that was growing on the side of the road around there was suddenly directly in front of me. I was bouncing up and down, hitting my head on the roof, but managed to wrench the wheel just enough to glance off the tree and skid across the highway onto the grass on the opposite side of the road, and there we came to earth, foot jammed on the brake, in a great cloud of dust. The trailer was 30 feet back on the opposite side of the road, showing her underside to the world.

Pulling a face and rubbing my elbow, as the dust settled I glanced over to the trailer in a state of shock. This was a truck driver's nightmare. I could see a couple of the trailer wheels in the air, spinning slowly. The tarpaulin had ripped, and there were tyres scattered everywhere, all over the road and the grass, and some had bounced crazily over a farmer's fence and out into his paddock, hundreds of feet away. As I looked, the last one toppled over in the paddock and was hidden by the grass.

I was seething with anger and feeling guilty at the same time, disappointed that I had not been able to keep her on the road and upright. I wanted to murder that car driver, if only I could find him. I took stock of myself, flexing arms and legs. I only had a sore elbow; it must have flicked against the inside of the door. I was okay physically. Very lucky. I could have been killed by that stupid car driver. If I had hit the huge gum tree head-on it would have been the end for me.

I slowly climbed down from the cab and inspected the damage. There was wood from the tree jammed into the wheel nuts of the front wheel where I had hit it, and a few bruises and buckles to the cabin—not too bad. The prime mover was well off the road, and the trailer was sort of sideways down the slight bank but would not interfere with traffic.

The tyres gave me a problem. They would make good

pickings if I couldn't protect them. Some of the professional black marketeers were rough, but even normal local people at accidents back then thought that overturned trucks were fair game, that they were free to steal what they could get their hands on. I would have to gather and stack them near the trailer, away from the road. It was going to be a long night. I trudged up the road and started to bowl tyres over to the back of the trailer, then stacked them so that they couldn't be seen by any motorists driving towards the bend. Viewed from the other direction, the overturned trailer was on a slight angle so the tyres, stacked close to it, would not be seen too easily. It took me about four hours to be satisfied that it was as good as could be. All the loose tyres were stacked in a heap where I could see them, beside the trailer and away from the road. When I finished I was in a lather of sweat.

I gave some money to the one car driver who came along while I was stacking the tyres and asked him to ring the boss and tell him where I was and what had happened. As the day progressed some of the few cars on the road slowed down and had a stickybeak, but no one bothered to ask if everything was okay or how the driver was—just looked briefly and drove on.

Towards late afternoon I took out a refrigerator cover I kept in the cabin and laid it out under the gum tree. It was like a sleeping bag, all padded. I slipped my .45 pistol inside and laid my Winchester rifle on top of the cover. I knew I was not going to have any sleep that night. I gathered some sticks and bits of wood so I could have one fire going all night near to where I had made my camp and another close to the tyres, about 30 feet away. With darkness came the cold. It was early spring and still chilly at night. In fact, I predicted there would be a frost in the morning, and there was. I changed into warmer clothes. Over the top I pulled on a leather jacket. I knew it would be next morning before the boss could arrive. It was a 400-mile run from Sydney to where I had come to grief.

Time dragged on. The couple of trucks on the road pulled up to see if they could help, were thanked and continued on their way. Then at about 8 pm a couple of cars cruised up slowly and quietly. I had an uneasy feeling that they knew I was there and what had happened, that they were planning to get up to mischief if they could. I watched as the cars gently stopped on the other side of the road and five or six men climbed quietly out into the darkness.

Up to then I had been lying down near the fire, but as the doors of the cars clicked open and shut, I slowly stood up. I leant back against the tree and cradled the Winchester in my left arm, a bit like a modern-day Davy Crockett. I could see the men, their cars and the tyres without having to move.

The group sauntered across the road into the firelight, all young except for one older man. 'Had a bit of trouble?' the older one asked. He was a tough-looking character, this one.

'Nothing I can't handle,' I replied, as I worked the Winchester's lever action with a flourish.

The young ones were more interested in the tyres. Two had moved quite close, bending down for a better look, trying to read the sizes. But at the sound of the rifle being cocked they quickly straightened up and turned around to look at me. The whole group stood stock-still, staring at me. No one moved.

'The cops are patrolling the road,' I announced loudly.

'Out this far?' the old guy asked with a surprised look on his face, while eyeing me up and down.

'Yeah. They know I'm here,' I replied.

The older man looked directly at the Winchester and quickly turned on his heel, calling out, 'Come on, boys.'

The rest followed him back to the cars. They huddled around, talking briefly among themselves for a minute or two, then the car doors opened and shut, and they drove off quietly, back the way they had come. I was sure they were up to no good. They certainly didn't offer any help, just took off into the night. I wondered what would have happened if I hadn't been nursing my trusty Winchester rifle. It had got me out of a few scrapes over the years.

They may come back later was my next thought. *Better stay awake.* I let out a sigh and cleared the rifle. The funny part was that I hadn't seen a policeman all day; I had been bluffing. Very seldom did the highway patrol come out this far into the bush. They mostly stayed around the town perimeters or just a few miles out.

At about 10 pm I heard a motorbike coming from the direction of Albury, the town down on the border. I guessed it was the police. Somebody must finally have told them about the overturned truck.

I was right. With a roar, a police bike skidded to a halt and a highway patrol officer idled down to where I was sitting by the fire. They were called the safety bureau in those days, the ones on bikes—helmets, goggles and so on. They rode Triumph Tiger 100s, which were very fast, could clock over 100 miles per hour.

'Bit cold, isn't it?' the officer said.

'Yeah,' I replied, looking casual and glancing down at the refrigerator cover, checking that he couldn't see the pistol. This was the first chance I'd had to tell anybody what had happened apart from the call to the boss, which I hoped the car driver had made.

The officer asked what happened, I told him, he nodded, and then he sat down on the refrigerator cover by the fire and put his hands out to warm them. He had to sit exactly on the lump that was my pistol, didn't he? 'Huh!' he said. 'Must be a rock.' And he moved his bum over a bit. I swallowed and didn't say a word. He pointed to the Winchester leaning against the tree. 'Had any problems?'

'Not really. Two car loads of young bucks pulled up a couple of hours ago and looked around. They eyed the tyres but went quietly when they saw the rifle.'

'Well, you seem to have everything under control. It's cold out here. I'm off home to bed.' With that he walked over to the bike, kickstarted it, adjusted his goggles and with a nod in my direction disappeared into the night.

Very helpful, I thought.

Two trucks pulled up during the night—the only traffic

on the road. Their drivers wished me well and hurried on. That was the sum total of interest in my predicament that night.

The boss arrived next morning. We transhipped the load and arranged for the truck and trailer to be towed to Albury and repaired.

●

Trees were my nemesis. In forty years of long-distance trucking I never touched another vehicle or person while driving—just trees.

My worst experience with trees happened in a Kenworth with an all-up weight of over 35 tons. My co-driver lost it on a bend, and we went bush at 50 miles an hour, demolishing forest trees for 200 feet or more before he could get it under control. We ended up a few feet away from a huge gum tree that would have killed us. I was petrified just hanging on and watching. Actually, it was then I decided that enough was enough.

Funny thing—I never had an affinity for wood. At school my woodwork teacher would throw my sample for end-of-year grading out the window, telling me to take it to the drycleaner's and get all the glue off so he could see what it was supposed to be. I was hopeless with wood.

By the way, the model of British Leyland truck I was driving that day was called a Comet.

19

Bank run

I was an owner-driver subcontracting for Wridgways Removals in Melbourne with a 1952 Commer furniture van that had a capacity of 30 tons. It was the usual practice for bank managers on their way up the scale of seniority to spend time out in the country towns, not staying too long in each place, so that the bank kept itself at arm's length from too much involvement with the locals. The bank managers would live in houses that belonged to the bank. Wridgways had a contract with the Commercial Bank of Australia, and when it was time to shuffle everyone around, a 'bank run' was started.

A furniture van would be loaded in Melbourne with a manager's belongings. When we arrived at the manager's new house, we would pack up all the personal belongings of the outgoing occupant into wooden tea chests, which we took out of the house with the furniture and put to one side, usually on the front lawn or, if it was raining, in the garage. We would then empty the van, taking the furniture and belongings from Melbourne into the house. When that was finished we loaded the van with the outgoing furniture and proceeded to the town where the second manager had been posted, and went through the same process as before. Sometimes there would be maybe two or three moves in the bank run, sometimes more, carried out over a number of days of constant loading, unloading and travelling between towns.

One time, my offsider and I had been going at it for about a week. In Mildura, after loading the final load, which was to be taken to Melbourne, I said I would need a sleep before we started. My offsider said he was feeling okay and would drive for a while.

In the front peak of the van, the part that sits out over the cabin, I'd had a trapdoor built so that one of us could sleep up there and one on the seat of the truck when we needed to. I climbed up into the peak, and with the movement of the truck I was asleep in no time.

Later on, my sleep was interrupted. I awoke in darkness and found myself sliding down into the left-hand corner of the peak, with the blanket over my head. I could hear the motor idling but there was no road movement. I started to grope around for the torch or the trapdoor but had great difficulty finding either. Nothing was where it should be, and everything was at the wrong angle. I couldn't get my bearings; I felt as if I were upside down. It was a bit of a worry there for a minute, scrambling around in the dark. I knew something was very wrong.

Finally, locating the trapdoor, I slid out awkwardly, sideways, into the cabin. The truck was on its side. It had slid off the edge of the road and down an embankment at a 45-degree angle; then as it had stopped it had tipped over gracefully onto its side, like a dying horse. The odds and ends strapped on the roof had scattered in the grass.

I started yelling at the offsider to turn the motor off. He was sort of mesmerised, hanging on to the steering wheel above me, and ready at any second to fall on top of me. His leg was jammed on the brake pedal, stopping him from falling, and he was just staring out into the darkness beyond the headlights, hanging on like grim death. He finally came back to earth, leant upwards, still hanging on like a tree dweller, and switched everything off.

It turned out he hadn't been as awake as he'd thought. We were about 20 miles from the town of Ouyen, not very far from Mildura. He had gone to sleep and drifted off the road, halfway down a steep embankment. It had been raining for days, and all the ground was soft; that's how she had slid down the bank and into a soft, muddy landing on her side. Luckily, we hadn't completely rolled over onto the roof, but it was mighty close.

Having the van on its side presented us with a problem beyond our capabilities. The next day we had to get the help of a local bulldozer, which pulled the van back onto its wheels and then tugged it through the mud up onto the road.

We must have been good packers, as there was no damage to the furniture. And there were only a couple of scrapes on the truck body, thanks to the rain and mud. We restacked the roof and made it back to Melbourne with no more mishaps.

Barrie Sculley

20

A night for guns

McNealy and Debney operated International 180s and one British Leyland diesel, all with 32-foot semitrailers with removable gate sides about 8 feet tall that slotted into the trailer's gunwale. When not in use they could be stacked under the trailer on a frame welded to the chassis. Loading tyres one at a time by hand took all day, slowly working away towards the rear of the trailer with car and truck sizes all mixed, usually between one and two thousand, stacking them row after row, higher than the gate sides. Each gate from the top centre rail was anchored with a double hitch to the tie rail on the opposite side, like a big 'X', to stop them bulging out. Then at the end of the day a couple of hours had to be spent tarping and roping down the high load. Even with the gate sides it ended up a floppy load that had to be tied down as tightly and firmly as was possible. Twenty-five to thirty ropes were needed with triple sheepshank knots. When finished it looked like a large covered wagon with an uneven top profile, unmistakably a truck with a load of new tyres.

One time I had loaded out of the Goodyear factory in Sydney, a full load of car and truck tyres destined for Melbourne. Loading had started at 8 am and finished about 5.30 pm. After tarping and tying, finally I was all set to go. Not back to the depot or home, but off into the cold, dark night. There was no time for a shower or a meal. I had to be at least 100 miles down the road before I could even think about dinner or a couple of hours' sleep. I would need all of the next day and part of the night to arrive on time in Melbourne the day after.

Leaving the bright city lights and plunging into the darkness, the headlights bouncing ahead, lighting up the narrow road, I pushed as hard as possible, swapping cogs and giving it to her to get up and over Razorback Mountain and to the little town of Mittagong in the Highlands. If I was lucky, the Greek cafe would still be open, the only one in that part of the country that might be. I was bloody hungry.

I knew that another load of tyres from the Dunlop factory would be around on the road somewhere—maybe behind, perhaps in front, and, even better, he might be at the cafe and we could keep each other company on the dangerous climb up Cuttaway onto the higher plain on the way to Goulburn, where there was a safe resting place for a few hours' sleep.

With force of habit I continually checked the small rear-view mirror, looking for a following vehicle that might be a sign of trouble. No side mirrors in those days. *So far so good*, I thought. No headlights behind, everything black.

I settled down to some serious driving, pushing her all the way. At last I topped Alpine Hill, and there were the lights of Mittagong straight ahead. My only thought then was, *Please let the cafe be open!* My tummy was rumbling. Off throttle, relax a little, glide past the Bowral turn-off and yes! It was still open. The lights inside were glowing out onto the road, beacons in the dark. Best of all, the Dunlop truck was outside, across the road from the cafe with room for me behind it.

I climbed down and walked across the road, seeing the driver inside by the window. He was at the best table, as he could see the trucks under the one streetlight across from the cafe. I was in luck: I knew him. 'G'day, Mac, how ya doin'?' I called across to him, as I pushed the door open and made my way to the counter.

'Could be better,' he replied with a long face.

I ordered a mixed grill, pulled my gloves off and sat down with him. 'What's the matter? The truck playin' up?' I asked.

'Nah, that's the least of my worries.'

I would have been surprised if he had said yes, as the International 180 with the Black Diamond motor that he and I were driving was a great all-round truck.

A slight pause.

'I know—girl troubles.'

'Yeah, I wish,' he replied. It was then I noticed that as he was eating he kept glancing out the window at his truck. He looked around the room and lowered his voice. 'You see any vehicles following you in the last hour, anything strange on the road?'

I instinctively looked out the window at the two trucks as well. 'No, the road's deserted,' I replied. 'Haven't seen a thing. Why?'

'I think I'm in a bit of trouble.'

'Like what?'

'They want to pinch the truck.'

'What? Who? Who wants to steal your truck?'

'Dunno.'

'Mac, start at the beginning, mate. What are you talking about?'

'Hang on,' he said, 'here comes a car.'

I could see headlights reflecting off my truck and getting brighter. A small car went past. It looked like one person driving. I glanced back across the table at Mac. He was intently watching the car; then as it disappeared into the darkness he looked at me. 'They want the tyres,' he said, nodding towards his truck. I looked blankly at him then frowned. 'Ray, it's true, mate. They want to steal my truck for the tyres. Probably sell 'em on the black market.'

It was a time when shortages were common, and many commodities were unobtainable or in short supply, causing a black market to spring up. People were willing to pay twice as much as normal and even more for hard-to-find goods and would not ask too many questions about where they had come from. This encouraged the ungodly, criminal types to run rampant, stealing and reselling anything that could make black money for them. Tyres were near the top of the list. They were called 'black gold' in those days—hard to get and easy to sell.

I said, 'You mean there is someone out there waiting to steal your truck?'

'Yeah, somewhere. Out there.'

I felt a cold tingle down my spine. 'Mac, you're giving me the jitters. Hang on. I'll be back in a minute.' I ran out of the door, yelling at the cook, 'Back in a minute!' I ran across the deserted road, anxiously swivelling my head, looking up and down the road as far as I could see.

I opened the door, and reached over and grabbed my pistol from under the towel on the seat. I checked the magazine was full and nothing was up the spout, put the safety catch on and jammed it into the top of my pants, then quickly pulled my jacket over it. I then strolled slowly back across the street, glancing from left to right, trying to penetrate the darkness for anything unusual. It was not as if I was used to this sort of situation, but with Betsy in my belt I knew no one was going to steal *my* load of tyres too easily.

'What's up?' said Mac as I sat down again, glancing out the window.

'Nothing. Now tell me all about it. How are they going to steal your truck?'

'This morning at smoko I went to the cabin to get my cigarettes. There was a typewritten note on the seat. Have a look.' He handed me a crumpled sheet of paper.

I smoothed it out and started to read. 'Leave your truck unlocked when you stop to eat. Wait an hour to report truck missing. It will be parked on a busy street in two days, unharmed.' I slowly raised my head and looked at Mac. 'Is this for real, Mac, or someone playing a joke?'

'Don't bloody know, but it's a worry, isn't it? What to do?'

We both looked out the window again as lights flickered on the rear of my truck. I had started my meal but put the knife and fork down to reach under my jacket. The feel of Betsy was more worrying than comforting.

The car, a small canvas top, just motored past, indifferent to our anxious faces looking at it from the cafe.

'Have you told the police?'

'No. What can they do? It's too vague—doesn't say where or when. It's nearly six hundred miles to Melbourne, and through two states . . .'

I finished my meal, or as much as I could eat under the circumstances. 'Have you got a gun?' I asked.

'Yeah, a twenty-two, but no shells.'

I didn't carry a .22, so I couldn't help him with that. 'I have a Winchester you can borrow.'

He looked at me with a solemn face. 'Okay, thanks. Don't know whether I want it. You know—what are we getting into here?'

'We are truck drivers, Ray, freight movers. It's tough enough fighting the government, the police and the transport inspectors for a fair go. We don't need these bastards as well. It's not fair, mate.'

He was silent for a bit, then said, 'Damn it. Give us a lend of the Winchester. Bugger them; they're not going to get my tyres, the bastards.'

'Okay,' I replied. 'Tell you what. If we get going now, we can make Goulburn in a couple of hours or so, park outside the police station and get a few hours' sleep. I'll keep close behind you all the way. I don't think we'll have a problem tomorrow in daylight. By then we should be well out of range of any Sydney heavies.' Mac nodded. We both looked out the window again for about the twentieth time. 'Come on. Let's do it.'

We paid for the meal and walked out onto the street. I kept half a pace behind Mac, with my right hand tucked under my jacket, firmly gripping Betsy. We stopped at the edge of the pavement, looking both ways into the darkness. All was quiet; it was just us and our trusty chariots out there in the cold. A little fog was starting to drift around the streetlight.

I ran across the road, saying, 'I'll get you the Winchester. Don't shoot yourself in the leg or something, okay? The Winchester is different from a twenty-two.' I chuckled, opening the door. His .22 was a bolt action, easy to work in close quarters. The Winchester was a lever action, needing a bit of space to lever and load it. I pulled it out, showing him the action and warning him not to have his finger inside the

177

guard, as he might accidentally discharge it, snapping the lever shut and blowing his passenger-side window to bits.

Another quick look up and down the street, a pat on the shoulder, and he ran up to his truck, holding the rifle at the ready. I yanked Betsy out of my pants and laid her on the seat, on top of the towel this time. I pressed the starter button, switched the lights on and waited.

A puff of exhaust, then Mac's lights came on and away we rolled. I followed closely behind.

Just out of town was a long, steep climb—a low-gear job from the bottom to the top. I eased in behind Mac, nearly stopping, and then we both started the grind to the top, up the narrow bit of sealed road that was called a highway in those days. We weren't overloaded and knew we could make it without any trouble. Unless trouble came from somewhere else. With that thought in mind I felt down and touched Betsy again.

That slow climb was a nightmare. I couldn't keep my head still, looking in the rear-view mirror and then watching that I didn't creep up on Mac in front. If I stalled going up there I'd have big trouble attempting to get her going again. I'd probably snap an axle, and wouldn't that be great.

I heaved a sigh of relief as we reached the top, and off we went, two covered wagons bouncing through the forest, then out into the open country, not about to stop for anyone or anything.

It had been a long day, and I was tired, but the adrenalin pushed me on till the lights of Goulburn welcomed us. We hadn't seen a soul, not a car or a truck the whole way. It was with relief that we parked outside the police station, which had a light on. I locked the door and promptly fell asleep.

•

Mac woke me at dawn and we had a cigarette, standing on the road in the morning mist. 'What do you reckon?' he asked.

'Dunno.' Then, with a deep sigh, looking up and down the road, I said, 'Okay then, let's make a mile.'

Mac nodded. We climbed into our trucks and hit the starter buttons.

As the miles rolled on so the tension seemed to ease away. The sun was shining brightly, and the dark night's fears were yesterday's. We stayed together all the way to Melbourne and never had a problem, nothing out of place.

When unloaded we met at the Waterside Hotel for a drink. The guns were safely hidden away, back where they belonged, and we wondered what it had all been about. There had been a few successful hijacks back then, so it was normal for us to be wary, especially with such a rich haul of tyres. Had it been a joke or the real thing? We never found out.

21

Fast and furious in the USA

A couple of months before my seventieth birthday, in October 2000, I decided to go to the USA for a holiday—I planned to buy a car and travel around to wherever took my fancy. I was determined to experience everyday life, so I joined Hostelworld, even though I wasn't young any more in age; in my heart I was twenty-one again. I decided to go with Japan Airlines and had a very enjoyable trip via Tokyo.

On arrival in Los Angeles I stayed at Backpackers Paradise Hostel, whose swimming pool, rooms, staff and amenities were all great. And it cost a fraction of the price of a room in a hotel. I stayed in many hostels such as this all over the USA and found them great value. I was made very welcome, even though I was an oldie.

Unable to buy a suitable car in Los Angeles, I decided to fly to San Francisco and try there. But when I arrived I saw a 'drivers wanted' advertisement on the message board in the hostel at Fort Mason, just up the road from the famous Fisherman's Wharf, and presented myself to the car delivery firm in question. My Australian drivers licence plus an international drivers licence were sufficient to be offered a car to deliver to Seattle, in Washington state, up near the Canadian border through northern California and Oregon. The first tank of fuel was free; all I paid was the cost of the fuel for the trip after that.

After depositing $300 as a bond refundable on delivery I set out in a late-model Mercury, and that was the start of a most wonderful and enjoyable journey, seeing and talking to everyday people who made me welcome wherever I went.

I eventually delivered the car to an army base in Seattle, then went into town. I stayed at the Hostelling International Seattle Hostel for a week, after which I was offered another delivery, of a turbocharged Saab to St Louis, way down in Missouri. However, I decided to have a few days in Vancouver and took the Green Tortoise Bus, a little Toyota HiAce for tourists, which gave me the chance to see the scenery.

Strangely enough, Canadian immigration was the only place I have ever been closely scrutinised, and they took their time in issuing me with an entry permit. I found this a little amusing, as over the years I had travelled to Indonesia, Japan, Hawaii, the USA, the UK and Mexico, and no one had ever looked twice at me before.

The cold in Vancouver was a bit much; it was spring, but the cold sliced through this old body, so after a week I decided, *No, time to find warmer places.* I went to a car auction, but nothing caught my fancy. While I was walking down the street wondering what to do a man approached me carrying a white plastic shopping bag full of crumpled clothes. He was dressed tidily and didn't look like a bum . . . Wrong, Ray. He breezed up, opening the bag for me to see the clothes inside, and said, 'I'm two dollars short to get my dry-cleaning done. Can you give me two dollars?'

Being a seasoned traveller I didn't hesitate, just kept walking, and threw a 'No' over my shoulder.

Okay, flying will be quicker, I decided, there and then.

There was a flight with Alaska Airlines leaving for Seattle that morning. I threw my clothes into a bag and managed to arrive at the airport just in time to buy my ticket and make the flight. Hurrying after the other travellers out onto the tarmac I viewed the jet with its white fuselage and large black lettering and thought, *Not many passengers. That's good. Plenty of seats—I'll get a window.* Little did I know why there weren't many passengers.

In fact, there were only six or eight of us on board. We were off the ground quick smart. When we reached cruising height the stewardess came down the aisle with a big smile on her face, offering newspapers and magazines to read. I accepted a newspaper. As I opened it with a flourish to the first page, my mouth dropped open, and I think I stopped breathing for a second or two. My eyes were reading what my brain didn't want to know. The headline filling the whole page boldly announced, 'Alaska Airlines Aircraft to be Grounded Due to Lack of Maintenance'. The article began, 'The horrific crash of an Alaska Airlines aircraft into the ocean off Los Angeles last week killing all on board is being investigated. Questions are to be asked about the poor maintenance and passenger safety'.

With a deep breath, I laid the paper down gently on my knees and stared around in a state of shock, then looked at the few heads I could see above the seats. *There doesn't seem to be any panic*, I thought. *Everything is quiet.* I wondered, *Are they all reading this?* I swivelled my head, looking around again.

I stared once more at the headline, my mind whirling with all sorts of thoughts. *Why didn't I know about this? What am I doing here? Why is this plane even flying if there are problems with maintenance?* I loved flying, had been in all sorts of aircraft since the 1940s, even at one time in the 1950s flying planes myself. I looked around the cabin again, perhaps expecting to see wild-eyed passengers running in panic up and down the aisle, or buzzing for oxygen. But no, I only saw the hostess, still smiling brightly, still handing out to right and left our possible death sentences. *I wish she would stop bloody smiling* was my next thought.

Turning my head away with a sinking feeling, I looked out of my window down to the ground, way, way below— about 30 000 feet below. It was a long way down. *Was that a bump? Was it? No.* Eyes swivelling, right to left and back again, nonstop. *No.* My eyes were drawn back to the view from the window, to that never-ending wilderness far below. I thought, *No one will ever find us.* I swallowed with difficulty and took another few deep breaths. My next thought: *Will I be buried in British Columbia, Canada, or Washington state in the USA? I guess it will depend on how far we travel before we fall out of the sky.*

I'd always wanted to spend a long time in the USA, but not this way, not forever. I decided to close my eyes and just think about nothing, and then it would all go away. *This can't happen to me, not me, no. Not to me, not now. It's not fair. The actual flight time is only about an hour. Why didn't I take that bloody Saab to St Louis?* I went through a checklist of what I could do if we crashed. *Where are the exits? Okay, I see them. Yep, one's close. Perhaps if I time it right I can leap into the air on impact. Hm, don't think that will work somehow; I'm sure to not get the sequence right. Well, it's obvious that it wouldn't work, dopey. Pipe down and shut up.*

The 'fasten seatbelts' sign came on. *This is it then,* I thought, looking out the window. *Brace yourself, Raymond. This is it. Now, be brave. Whatever you do, don't wet your pants. Yeah, yeah, shut up. Don't think about it.* The nose dropped and we started to descend very quickly. With my nose pressed against the window I carefully examined the wing and motor. They both seemed to be okay. The wing wasn't falling off, and the motor wasn't smoking, but the damn plane was losing altitude fast, very fast.

All of a sudden, out of nowhere, the ground came up to meet us—my heart beat faster—and then a chirp and a loud bump. I blinked a couple of times, and the cement runway was flashing past below my window. We had landed! We were on the ground, rumbling up to the terminal at Seattle Airport.

My thoughts ran wild. *We made it! We are on the ground, not in the air, you beaut! Well, you can blow a tyre or drop a bloody wing off now; I don't bloody care. I'm out of here. I wonder where the toilets are? Not far, I hope.*

Would you believe it, the hostess still had her smiling death mask on at the door as she wished us goodbye and have a lovely day. *No thanks to you lot,* I thought, as I hurried as quickly as I could away from that big white bird. In my haste to quit the scene I forgot to take the newspaper as a souvenir. The rattly airport bus into Seattle was a soothing relief, and quite a few drinks were had that night.

•

A couple of days later I did start for St Louis with the Saab and had a great trip dodging KWs (Kenworth trucks) and such over the Rocky Mountains. At one point I ran out of daylight and towns so had a restless night sleeping in the car at the Little Bighorn, South Dakota. I think I was communicating with Custer and the 7th Cavalry all night, thinking, *Mate, you also made mistakes like me, didn't you? But your last one was a humdinger. Fancy taking on thousands of Indians with seven hundred cavalry. I have yet to make such a large blunder, but give me time, give me time.*

The drive over the Rocky Mountains and through Idaho, Montana, Wyoming and South Dakota, then moving from mountains and forests to the plains of Nebraska, Kansas and

Missouri, was absolutely great. One little incident was amusing. Just near the top of the Rockies I caught up with a couple of Kenworth Tankers. They were moving at a fair rate, and I cruised past them and over the top onto a level piece of road. The next instant I looked in my rear-view mirror and all I could see was a big Kenworth badge filling the whole of my back window. Being an old interstate truck driver, I laughed: many times I had done the same to slow drivers. And so I waved them around. We were all clipping along at about 70 miles an hour.

•

A few hours out of Kansas City and soon after I had fuelled the car a warning light lit up on the dashboard, so I pulled over, checked the handbook, no answer. I checked water, oil, tyres and anything I could think of that might have triggered this warning light. Everything appeared normal. Damn. I decided to make a detour into Kansas City and check with the Saab agents.

Pulling off the highway I ended up in the industrial part of town, all factories and no public telephones to be seen. I wandered up a back street looking for a telephone and noticed a small tin shed on a block of land with a number of cars being washed and detailed outside. I stopped and walked in to ask for a telephone book.

A middle-aged man who was polishing a car was most helpful. He asked what was wrong and who I was trying to find. Then he described in detail how to get to the Saab agents:

I had to get back on the freeway, drive through the city, turn off the freeway after some distance, make a few more turns and I would be there. Halfway through his directions he had lost me completely. I asked whether, if he had the time and I paid him for his effort, he could take me there. He said he had to deliver the car he was cleaning just near to where I wanted to go, so I could just follow him.

What followed was for me hair-raising and for all the American drivers watching very interesting. Off he went in this black Cadillac, at what seemed like 1000 miles an hour, up a ramp onto a freeway with five lanes chock-full of traffic, driving like a rocket, weaving in and out of the lanes, with me trying not to lose sight of him, forcing my way into small spaces after him at 50 miles per hour, never taking my eyes off him, while waving my hand out of the window to tell him to slow down, worried I would end up two states away. But the black Cadillac ignored me completely.

We had been weaving in and out of traffic like this for about twenty minutes or so, an old man in a Saab honking the horn continually, blinking his headlights up and down, making hand gestures, intently chasing a Cadillac—what a sight for those around us in the traffic. The mind boggles at what they might have been thinking. I didn't have time to wonder, though, because suddenly the Cadillac dived down a ramp, with me hot on his tail, into a suburb where the road was much quieter. I stopped honking the horn and started to breathe easily again. What a ride! My guide pulled up outside the Saab agents with a huge grin on his face.

I gratefully paid him and told him it was the best money I had ever spent.

It was now 4 pm on a Friday afternoon, and I didn't like the idea of spending the weekend in Kansas City, so I drove the Saab up into the service area the wrong way, so that no one could get in or out. Immediately, I was rushed at by people in dustcoats waving their arms for me to move. One asked, 'Can I help you, sir?'

'No,' I said, 'but that needs help,' pointing to the Saab.

'What's wrong?'

'You tell me. For the last hundred miles it's had a red light on the dash telling me something is wrong. Damned if I can find it. I've checked water, oil, tyres—can't find what is wrong. It has to be in St Louis in a couple of days.'

After a quick check by three or four dustcoats I was informed that the light was only to tell the owner that the car was overdue for a service. Bloody hell. That was a relief. I was then asked politely to remove myself and the Saab, as I was blocking the entrance. That I did very smartly, telling the car to 'bloody behave yourself till I get you home'.

●

In due course I delivered the car a day early, even though I had been given plenty of time for sightseeing on the way. As I approached the house, up a long, winding driveway, I wondered at such a rich family having a little Saab, but it turned out it belonged to the daughter, who had been on holiday in Seattle. According to her mother she never looked after it as she should. The lady of the house then insisted on driving me into town in her Cadillac to the car delivery office to collect my money. As she brought the car around from the garage I retrieved my suitcase from the Saab and, with no one looking, gave the rear tyre a kick, remembering how I'd checked everything back on that lonely highway in the middle of nowhere, worried I had damaged something and that I would lose my deposit, and then the wild drive through Kansas City, tailing that black Cadillac. I muttered to it, 'See? Don't mess with me. You're home.'

Later in my trip I ended up in New York, at the NY Bed & Breakfast Hostel in Harlem. Wonderful staff made me feel very welcome. On a corner near to the main entrance of the hostel was a small deli, and every morning I bought a banana and yoghurt, then walked down the road to Central Park and sat on the grass, eating breakfast and watching the world go by.

Dinner at night was usually eaten overlooking Times Square, sitting at the window of a cute eatery with a hamburger and beer. One night I watched a crew setting up a movie scene in the middle of Times Square, but it was getting late so I have no idea what movie it was or who was in it!

I spent a week in New York and had a good wander around. I took the Staten Island Ferry and had a look at the Statue of Liberty, went to the World Trade Center, to the top floor, and admired the unbelievable views while having a drink or two—this was just one year before 9/11.

Then I travelled down to Florida by Amtrak. I arrived late at night, and the only place with vacancies was the Tropics Hotel and Hostel in Collins Avenue, opposite the beach. It was a great place to stay, with a full kitchen, large swimming pool and fantastic staff. I was there for 4 July, enjoyed coffee from an authentic Cuban coffee lounge and bought an antique Chinese vase as a memento.

From Florida I travelled by bus down through the Keys to Key West. I stopped at Key Largo for coffee and saw where the movie was made. Then I had my photo taken at the most southern point of the USA. I visited Ernest Hemingway's house—very Old World—and saw the wooden tower from which the original salvage operators watched for ships coming to grief on the shoals and reefs that surround Key West.

After a week I returned to Miami Beach and then took a Caribbean cruise to Mexico and back. After that I flew to New Orleans and enjoyed a few hectic nights in Bourbon Street, including the never-ending music—great. I also took a riverboat across the Mississippi and generally enjoyed my stay in the Deep South.

My advice? Grab your life with both hands and shake the best you can out of it. We've only got the one chance; don't waste it.

22

Static

Sometimes 'things' happened on the road, like the occasional breakdown or tyre trouble or a changed delivery address for the load. In fact, every second trip would have some sort of problem. In the 1950s we tried to avoid using telephones to communicate with head office, as it was too expensive. Whenever we could we'd instead send a telegram with minimal words, like, 'Tyre trouble ETA Wednesday am'. Sometimes, though, using a phone was unavoidable.

This bloke was a good driver and always punctual, but he was known as Static, because he stuttered very badly. If he was forced to use a telephone out in the sticks somewhere to contact the boss, it went like this: 'H-h-hullo, th-th-that you, boss?'

'Yeah. What's up?' from the boss.

'Th-th-the f-f-fuel f-f-filter keeps b-b-blocking up.'

All of this took quite some time to get through, and the seconds were ticking by, using up the driver's money. The operator would be warning him to put more money in the telephone, which Static wouldn't have, so the connection would be broken, with the boss left hanging on to an empty line wondering what he was supposed to do and, more importantly, whether Static and his truck were on their way again.

As time went on, if Static had to ring the boss for a delivery address, he was told to say 'It's me' and nothing else. The boss would know who it was and would immediately read out the delivery address, Static having been told to always have a pen and paper ready so he didn't have to say another word! They polished the system, and it worked okay. They managed to avoid telephone calls that ate up money and went nowhere.

23

Boomerang

One time in 1956, I was broken down out on the Nullarbor Plain, hundreds of miles from anywhere. I needed to get a lift into Ceduna; it was the nearest town, about 300 miles east from where I had come to a jarring halt. I thought of the cowboy in the old days when his horse broke a leg: he shot it, heaved his saddle onto his shoulder and trudged off towards civilisation. Looking at my huge, 30-ton monster I knew a bullet wasn't much use. I had no dynamite, and no insurance, so I had to try to fix it.

It was a long, hot, dry track out there, and when you broke down it seemed to get hotter and drier and more forbidding. I had been there for some days without anyone coming past, but I knew sooner or later a car or truck would materialise

Albion HD model and two AEC Matadors: typical workhorses for crossing the Nullarbor Plain in the 1950s.

out of the heat haze. If it was a car and had no spare seat then I would send a message with them; if a truck I knew I could squeeze in somehow.

Out there I always wore just a pair of navy-blue Speedo swimmers, to try to keep cool. But I had learnt that when doing some dirty work it was better to wear an old long-sleeved shirt and ex-army trousers over the top. The water I carried was for drinking only, not for cleaning hands or anything. If I covered up with clothes, at the end of the day it was only a matter of cleaning my hands with some dieseline and wiping them on a piece of rag, rather than having grease and oil all over my body and having to spend hours and gallons of dieseline trying to get clean again.

I had the radiator out and was standing at the front, leaning into the gap, unbolting the timing cover at the front of the motor. It was mid morning, the heat was already making me uncomfortable, and I was wishing I could be anywhere but where I was. It was deadly quiet, not a sound to be heard. Humming away to myself, intent on what I was doing, I suddenly had the feeling that someone was watching me.

I casually glanced over to my right, still undoing the bolt in the timing cover—nothing but the heat haze shimmering out there. Brushing the sweat from my forehead with my sleeve, I then glanced over my left shoulder and instantly froze. My hand stopped turning the wrench on the bolt, but then I quickly turned my head back to the motor and continued to unscrew the bolt, wondering all the time, *Where did* they *come from? Am I seeing things? What do I do now?*

They were a group of Aboriginals, six or seven of them, standing about a truck's length away. I hadn't heard or seen a thing. From my quick glance all I had taken in was a bunch of wild-looking, half-naked men armed with spears and boomerangs, staring at me. The spears looked long and sharp, and they were holding the boomerangs like clubs.

I continued to hum to myself, dismissing what I had seen and not wanting to have another look, hoping it would all disappear. My rifle and pistol were in the cabin, well away from me, and the only thing I had at hand was a large tension wrench, which I could use as a baton in self-defence if needed.

I knew there were a few wandering tribes of Aboriginals who made their home in the desert, but they were not seen very often. In all the years that I had been travelling back and forth across it I had never come across any. Back in the 1950s, Aboriginals were not citizens of Australia. There was no accurate record of their numbers. The average white Australian did not know much about them. We were aware that they wandered all the time, seldom stopping for long in the one place, that they were hunters and quite primitive by our standards.

I felt a presence very close to my back. My neck tingled. I swung around and warily eyed a young man who had come within arm's reach. He was slightly taller and heavier than me, holding a wicked-looking boomerang in his hand. He was staring over my shoulder into the motor compartment.

He turned his head ever so slightly, and our eyes made contact. I wondered what I should do if he made a threatening move. Grab for a gun? Run off into the desert? Offer a cigarette? Smile? Shake hands? But instead of threatening me, in what seemed a friendly gesture the tall man offered me the boomerang.

Maybe they are friendly, I thought to myself as I wiped my hands down my trouser legs. My mind still running at 1000 miles an hour, I took the boomerang, examining it, while trying to figure out what was happening. It was made of a type of mulga wood. I nodded very knowingly and handed the boomerang back. He then shook his head and thrust it back at me, which worried me for a second, but then it occurred to me that he was presenting it as if he was giving it to me.

Hm, I thought, *what can I give in exchange?* I could spare some water and a little food, not much, but no problem if they needed it. While this train of thought was going slowly through my brain, the man took the boomerang back. *Good. Maybe they will go now*, I thought hopefully. But he raised the boomerang into the air above his head, while my heart skipped a beat. In my mind's eye I saw my head split open and my brains dribbling over the timing cover that was proving so awkward to get off. He stepped back a little then raised a forefinger at me, seeming to say, 'Watch me.'

So I stood completely still and watched, at the same time thinking, *If he makes a threatening move I'll throw the wrench at him and make a run for the cabin.* He moved away from the truck, held the boomerang up in the air to attract my attention to it, and then threw it. It cartwheeled a little then fell to the ground. There was a murmur—it seemed of annoyance— and a rustle of movement from the group standing a little way off. The thrower ran and retrieved the boomerang, lashing the ground with it in temper a couple of times. That also made me a little uneasy, and I edged closer to the driver's door. Again, finger in the air to me, he launched it. Away it went, swishing out, then returned to him, falling at his feet. He picked it up and, finger in the air again, repeated the performance. Perfect.

He walked over and offered it to me. I took it and made the appropriate facial expressions, with raised eyebrows and nodding of head, as if I were an expert on boomerangs, then handed it back to him.

He thrust it towards me again, while I shook my head with my hands raised in front of me as a refusal. I then uttered the first words of this encounter, 'No baccy,' even though I'd had a cigarette in my mouth when they arrived. 'Got no baccy.'

He stood there looking at me then offered the boomerang again.

'What? What do you want?' I asked loudly, shrugging my shoulders.

He stretched his hand out towards me, grasped my trousers at the knee and shook them. He wanted my pants.

Is that all? I thought with relief.

It was then that I really looked at him and the others closely. I could see a worn-out blanket here and there. There were a couple of women wearing rag-like dresses, and six men, some old, with bits and pieces of clothing on. One had what looked to be an old coat, but there wasn't much left of it. My boomerang thrower had remnants of shorts tied around his waist with a piece of twine.

Without hesitation I dropped my trousers to the ground and handed them to him. (I'm not sure that I would have done so if I hadn't had the Speedos on underneath!) He promptly pulled them on, took a deep breath and managed to do up the top button. Because he was slightly heavier than me, the fly gaped open—no zippers in those days; trouser flies were all buttons. He had no hope of doing all the buttons up, but he didn't care. He turned and strutted back to the group, the fly on the trousers bulging open, the crease in his buttocks as tight as a ballet dancer's. I was hoping he didn't bend over too soon, because they would split in half and I didn't have any more to spare.

The group sat down and had a long discussion, and then very gingerly the boomerang thrower stood up, came over to me and handed me a spear. It had seen better days, having a broken end patched with gum. I shook my head, but he insisted, then turned and walked back to the group.

One boomerang and one old spear for a pair of old ex-army trousers. Done. I also gave the group some water and a tin of Irish stew, which I opened for them. They camped some distance away that night.

•

By the next day I knew what parts I needed from Sydney, but I would have to get word to the truck dealership. Late in the morning, wondering what to do, I looked west and thought I saw a dust cloud. Sure enough, around midday a truck came along, going east, and I decided to hitch a ride to Ceduna, where I could order what I needed from Sydney. When the driver had stopped and agreed to give me a lift, I asked him to wait while I locked the truck.

The wanderers were still there. I walked over to the boomerang thrower, got his attention and pointed to myself, then pointed to the other truck, then pointed east. Then I pointed to the sun and drew a mark in the dust, pointed again to the sun and made another mark in the dust, and so on for five marks. Then I held five fingers up in the air and pointed backwards and forwards, to the sun, then to each finger, emphasising the number five.

Next, I pointed to him and then my truck, pointed to my eyes then his eyes, then back to the truck. Then I put my hand out towards the truck and with my other hand smacked it down, to say 'don't touch' and repeated the 'eye only' signals.

The man grunted and twice said something that sounded like 'pronk' then lifted his hand to his mouth, as if he were drinking out of a bottle.

I thought to myself, *He wants plonk—wine, or liquor of some sort*. Back then it was six months' jail for a white man who gave intoxicating liquor to Aboriginals. I nodded.

•

I made it into Ceduna, ordered the parts and hitched a ride back to my truck in four days. The Aboriginals were still there. I examined the truck and tools—nothing had been touched.

The boomerang man came across and I opened two tins of Irish stew and gave them to him, along with a packet of Champion Ruby tobacco with papers, but he continued to wait expectantly. I had brought back two bottles of West End beer for me, so decided I'd give him one. *Can it do much harm*, I thought, *way out here in the middle of the Nullarbor Plain, hundreds of miles from nowhere?* It was obvious he had tasted liquor before. So I uncapped the second bottle and handed it to him. He immediately put it to his mouth and took a swig.

Next second he lowered the bottle and spat and blew good West End beer all over the ground. My West End beer! My one of only two bottles of West End beer, which I had nursed for the last two days and a night. He proceeded to wave the bottle around and peer at it, angrily shouting, 'Pronk, pronk!' It was the most noise I had heard out there since the two trucks had come past. It seemed that he wanted sherry or port—something sweet and strong.

This turn of events alarmed me a little, so I quickly walked to the truck, unlocked it, reached up under the bunk and strapped my .45 around my waist. The man was still raving and shouting as he walked back to the group sitting on the ground. I went some distance away from them, and, with my back towards them, I drew my pistol and started taking pot shots at an old Irish stew tin that I had thrown out some time ago. I completely ignored the group but managed to watch them out of the corner of my eye. When next I turned around they were moving slowly northwards, back into the desert and the ever-present heat haze.

They had not been threatening; in fact, they were helpful. They had appeared out of the northern desert and slowly disappeared back into it. After a couple of hours I lost sight of them in the shimmering heat. I was there for weeks after that, but I didn't see them again.

●

When I finally got home, my mother took the spear and used it as a curtain rod for years, but it was lost over time and with changing houses. The boomerang had pride of place on a shelf in the lounge room, prompting the story of its origin to be told over and over again, much to my embarrassment.

Then tragedy struck: the poor boomerang was murdered. One morning, after about twenty years of the boomerang being a talking point in our family, my eldest daughter, Sharron, asked if she could take it to school for a 'show and tell'. The poor kid didn't want to come home that night: the class went to the surf beach that afternoon and their young know-it-all teacher said he would show them how to throw a boomerang. In spite of Sharron's objections, he threw it out over the surf into the strong sea breeze. It circled, as a boomerang should, but returned with the speed of a jet liner over the children's heads, crashing into the rocks at the back of the beach and splintering to pieces. The teacher said it wasn't a proper boomerang, as it didn't return to the thrower.

On hearing the story I was tempted to correct his 'expert' knowledge but in the end decided to let it pass, so the perpetrator of the crime was never brought to justice.

I had never attempted to throw the boomerang in all those years I'd had it. Perhaps it decided it was time to go home, after being cooped up inside on a shelf for such a long time. It returned to where it had originated—the earth.

24
The ringing of the bell

Les Harris was a big, tall, solid fellow; he sort of looked down from on high, if you know what I mean. He was about forty years of age, ex-navy and a good shot with a pistol, and he had a great sense of humour—he was always ready for a joke.

Around 1958, soon after the new weighbridge operated by the Victorian Country Roads Board was opened at Seymour, about 60 miles north of Melbourne, Les was wandering down the road from Sydney to Melbourne called the Hume Highway. Sounds impressive, doesn't it? But it was just a narrow sealed road that meandered from town to town and eventually reached Melbourne, nearly 600 miles later. Les had a legal load and stopped for a chat here and there, checking what was going on down the road. That was the only way we knew what was around: talking to drivers coming the other way—no luxuries like telephones or CB radio back then—and that's when Les heard about this new weighbridge and how it operated.

It was a cement-block building with bullet-proof glass windows and a heavy steel door located on about a quarter of an acre well back from the road at the bottom of a slight hill. It was intended that the whole of that area would be used when the board was having a blitz, shutting down the highway completely and directing all trucks in for search and inspection. (We learnt later that if we switched our head-lights off and coasted down the hill we could sometimes slip past, if they were busy with a few trucks in line being weighed.)

Stopping at Joe's Service Station at Wodonga, on the Victorian border, for a cup of coffee, Les got talking to a driver who had just arrived from Melbourne and had been a candi-date for the new weighbridge. The driver had been instructed to drive his truck onto the weighbridge, stopping first to weigh the front axle and then, when the weighbridge opera-tor rang a bell, driving forwards and stopping to weigh the drive axle. Then, when the bell sounded again, he had to move on and stop with the trailer axle on the scales. If an axle was over the limit no bell rang, but the operator would walk around to the front of the truck and call the driver into the weighbridge office to view the scales and see how much he was overloaded by while they booked him. Les wasn't worried, as he was legal this trip and there were no warrants out for his arrest—he hadn't been a bad boy for quite a while.

The miles slipped away, and the night's darkness descended around him. As he approached Seymour he was advised by the blinking of headlights coming the other way that trouble was waiting up ahead. One driver turned his lights out momentarily and pointed to Les's wheels as he went past. Les thanked him by turning his own lights off quickly and continued unafraid into the spider's web ahead. His main thought was *Maybe I can have a bit of fun.*

Sure enough, as he approached the new weighbridge he saw the lights on and a couple of figures moving around inside the building. He was waved in to be weighed by a uniformed figure at the side of the road whom he recognised. Stopping a short distance away on the approach to the weighbridge, he leant out of the window as Charley Sinclair, the police sergeant attached to the Roads Board, walked up to the cabin and explained the procedure of this new weighbridge. Now, Charley was an understanding guy, what you would call a good copper, but he was still a policeman and on the 'other side'. He was in charge of all arrest warrants, keeping a small filing cabinet in his car, plus he had a good memory for faces and names. You never knew when Charley was going to show up in his unmarked Ford, as he wandered all over the state.

'You are to place each axle on the weighing platform one at a time,' he said to Les, 'and when the operator is satisfied he will ring a bell and you will move the next axle onto the bridge, and so on. Got it?'

As the instructions continued, Les leant out of the cabin, a hand cupped around his ear, overacting a little, nodding here and there as Charley shouted up his instructions.

When the bell was mentioned, Les looked vaguely down at Charley and asked, 'Bell? What bell? I can't see a bell anywhere.' Les looked out past Charley and around the wide cleared area, as if looking for a type of school bell, on a wooden tower somewhere out in the darkness.

'No, no, not out there; it's on the outside wall above the door of the building,' said Charley, pointing to the weigh-bridge office on the other side of the truck.

'I won't hear a tinkly bell in here, with all the noise this bastard makes.'

'You'll hear it, driver. Now move onto the bridge and remember to follow the instructions exactly, by the bell.'

Les drove onto the weighbridge, not stopping for the front axle but continuing on to put the drive axle on the scales.

Charley had walked behind the trailer and into the weigh-bridge office before he noticed that Les had the drive axle on the bridge instead of the front axle. With a sigh of exaspera-tion he stormed out of the office and around to the front of the truck, stopping under Les's window and looking up at Les with a frown on his face.

But before he could say a word, Les yelled down to him, 'I told you I wouldn't hear a bloody bell above this noise.'

'I haven't rung the bell yet,' said Charley.

'Well, what the hell's wrong?' asked Les.

'You have to put the front axle on first, for me to weigh it. Then I'll ring the bell.'

'But up the road they never bother with the front axle; it's impossible to overload it on a Mercedes-Benz 315.'

'I know that,' snapped Charley, 'but I want the weight of the whole load.'

'Oh, okay, okay,' said Les with a resigned look on his face. With a swoosh of released air from the trailer brakes, he very slowly reversed until his front axle was on the weighbridge. At the same time, he turned his radio up loud, seeking a station amid all the crackling. The bell rang, but Les ignored it, fiddling with the station knob on the radio. The bell rang again.

Next minute, Charley was waving his arms at Les through the passenger window, then, in a fit of temper, running around the front of the truck, past the headlights, to the driver's door again, shouting louder now. 'Didn't you hear the bell?'

'Eh?' said Les. 'Hang on.' He turned the radio down. 'What did you say?'

'Turn your radio off and listen for the damn bell, and when you hear it, move onto the next axle. All right? I haven't got all night to waste with you,' yelled Charley, starting to lose it a little. Charley knew there were trucks slipping past in the darkness out on the road, and he wanted to weigh as many as he could. All that time trucks had been going past in both directions, up and down the highway, and you can bet your sweet life that there were plenty of sighs of relief as they skittled past, going like the hammers of hell, drivers thanking their lucky stars it wasn't them on the bloody new weighbridge.

Les, well aware of what was going on around him, was trying to milk the opportunity for as long as he could without going just that bit too far; it was something he was a master at.

Charley turned and hurried back into the office, and after a moment the bell clanged. Les put the truck into gear and moved it up to the drive axle. A short wait, and the bell went off again. Les moved the truck forwards to put the trailer axle on the bridge. A short time later the bell sounded once more. Silence. The bell rang again. It was completely ignored by Les. Relaxed, elbows on the steering wheel and cupped hands holding his chin, looking out into the night, listening to that bell ringing its head off and half smiling to himself, there sat our Les.

Next second, Charley was round again, underneath the driver's window, jumping up and down, waving his arms. 'Didn't you hear the bell?' he shouted angrily. He was livid.

'Yeah, I heard the bell, but I've got no more axles, have I?' said Les, turning his head slowly and staring down at Charley, with a slight twitch of the mouth and an otherwise blank look on his face.

A few seconds went by, each man looking at the other.

Suddenly, Charley glanced over his shoulder as another noisy truck rumbled past on the highway. He turned back to Les, then, with a knowing look and half a smile, he jerked his thumb over his shoulder. 'Get going, driver.'

Once more a swoosh of trailer brakes, a slight crunch of gears, and Les, with a huge smile on his face, trundled down off that new weighbridge. Watching Charley in the rear-view mirror, hands on hips, standing in front of that new building with the bell, the opposition's latest weapon in the war of the highways, Les smiled to himself again, knowing he would be a marked man for a while.

And so the Great Game continued between the truckers and the enemy.

A Mercedes-Benz 315 similar to Les Harris's, from Jack Seaton's Transport, with (left to right) Ray Gilleland, Don Barnard and Frank Catlin.

25

The rabbit

Sam arrived home at about 10 pm. It was so great to be back after a lousy trip in which everything had gone wrong. He had a shower and a late supper, then went to bed, uttering a sigh of relief as he eased his way between the sheets, not wanting to disturb Ethel, his wife. He was looking forward to a couple of days of doing nothing.

They lived in a medium-priced suburb, the usual three-bedroom house with garage, a front lawn that seemed to always need mowing and a large backyard with outdoor table and chairs and an above-ground swimming pool for the kids. All the neighbours had similar properties, the backyards separated by wire or wooden fences. When it had been suggested that the kids needed a pet he had been all for it, thinking a

German shepherd dog would be just the thing. But, no, Ethel had had other ideas. Her option was a little terrier more suited to their backyard, and so that's what they got. Sam didn't like little terriers, but he was away a lot so it was best to give in to Ethel's wishes.

After a good night's sleep, at about lunchtime the next day Sam was leaning on the kitchen bench, drinking a cup of coffee and gazing out of the window at the backyard, trying to decide if he could leave the lawn for another week before mowing it. He didn't want to do anything but sit and watch a bit of television, maybe have a drink down the club later on—just relax. He had looked forward to this all the way home. Why find something to do to spoil his relaxation? The lawn could wait.

That was when he noticed Scamp, the terrier, in the yard, growling and flinging a grey something in the air and catching it. Sam couldn't see what it was—maybe a slipper or one of the kids' stuffed toys. Scamp was always quick to take advantage of any toys left around, and all the better if they were soft and cuddly. He loved to throw them about, growling, and to worry them by vigorously shaking his head from side to side with them in his mouth. Sam had lost a slipper or two that way.

As Sam was lost in reverie, Ethel sidled up to him with her cup of coffee and said, 'What are you smiling at?'

'Scamp. Look at him having fun with that grey fluffy toy. Or is it one of the kids' slippers?'

Ethel looked out of the window. Suddenly, she stiffened

in alarm. 'Oh my God. Sam, quick, get it off him. It's not a toy; it's next door's pet rabbit. Quick, quick! Oh no!' Ethel dropped her cup and ran for the back door with Sam in pursuit, finally realising something was dreadfully wrong.

They shooed Scamp away, who was not too happy about giving up his plaything but went back to demolishing an old slipper nearby, ignoring the fuss going on around him.

'What are we going to do? The Browns loved their rabbit—it was such a pet,' said Ethel, gazing down at the little grey body lying there on the lawn, all crumpled. 'Scamp, look what you've done!' she yelled at the dog, who was not taking a bit of notice.

The rabbit was kept in a wire hutch on the Browns' back lawn so they could move it around and the rabbit could always have a nice grassy area to live on. Damn the dog; it had always wanted that rabbit. Sam and Ethel had been warned many times about Scamp barking and trying to dig under the fence to get at the rabbit, and Sam had always been shooing Scamp away from the fence and filling in the holes he had made. But finally the dog had made it.

Sam picked up the dead rabbit; it was covered in Scamp's saliva and wet mud from where he had burrowed under the fence. The cuddly rabbit was a dirty, soggy, pitiful mess.

'What are we going to do?' said Ethel. 'Jean and Bill are at work. They won't be home till about five. How can we tell them that Scamp got in there and killed their rabbit?'

Sam replied, 'Can we buy another one and slip it into the cage?'

'I don't know where we could get one at short notice like this.' Ethel reached over, took the rabbit from Sam and closely examined it. 'There's no blood or open wounds,' she said thoughtfully. 'It must have died of shock.' She gazed out over Sam's shoulder, her brain going at 100 miles an hour, as only a woman's can do. 'Sam, how about we clean it up and put it back in the cage as if nothing had happened? We can fill in the hole under the fence. The Browns will think it just died naturally. We'll be off the hook, and Scamp won't be blamed.'

Sam looked at Ethel. 'Do you think we could get away with it?'

'It's worth a try,' said Ethel. 'Come on; time's getting away.'

And so the makeover began. First they took the rabbit into the laundry and gently washed it in warm, soapy water, being very careful not to leave a speck of dirt on its coat.

'Now what?' asked Sam, looking at his watch.

'Quick,' said Ethel, 'into the bathroom.'

Sam followed Ethel into the bathroom, gently carrying the dead, wet, but clean rabbit. Ethel opened a drawer and took out the hair dryer, and while Sam slowly and gently rotated the rabbit she gave it a blow-dry.

After about fifteen minutes, the rabbit was dry. It looked like it was sleeping, all soft and cuddly. The difference between the dirty, grubby little thing they had rescued from Scamp and this fluffy, grey and white rabbit was amazing.

'Okay,' said Ethel, 'now you run next door and plonk it

in the cage. Lay it out like it's asleep. Hurry—they will be home soon.'

Sam did as instructed, even rearranging it a couple of times to get it just right. Then he went back home. Checking his watch, he quickly filled in Scamp's hole under the fence. He looked across at the hutch in the Browns' backyard, thinking, *Yep, looks good. No one will ever know.*

After such a hectic time, Sam and Ethel decided a drink was needed. And not tea or coffee: Ethel had two large glasses of red wine, and Sam had a double scotch.

A short time later, all hell broke loose in the Browns' backyard, with a lot of hysterical screaming and yelling. Ethel looked out of the kitchen window with a guilty expression on her face, not daring to move. Sam ran out to the fence and looked over it. There was Jean Brown, wide eyed, looking around their backyard with her hand to her mouth. Bill, her husband, was leaning on the hutch with his mouth open, staring down at the cuddly grey rabbit, then slowly gazing around the yard, and then back at the rabbit, shaking his head from side to side, not believing what he was seeing.

'What's the matter? Somebody hurt?' Sam called out to them, leaning on the top of the fence with genuine concern written all over his face.

'Our rabbit's dead in the hutch,' said Bill loudly, as Jean slowly sank to the grass, all white and trembly, her eyes starting to roll back in her head.

'Well, mate, I suppose these things happen sometimes,' Sam called out as kindly as he could.

Bill looked at Sam, then around the yard, and then back at Sam, and said, in a hushed voice, 'Yeah. But it died two days ago, and we buried it down near the back fence.'

Sam went looking for Ethel.

George Johnston

26

Terracotta warrior

This young fellow worked in the yard and on the local trucks, but he wanted to get on the interstate run. As time went on, though, he despaired of ever getting a chance, until, out of the blue one day, the foreman said, 'Slip home and pack your bags. You're off to Adelaide tonight.'

He was a good driver, excited about his first trip interstate, and he managed quite well down the highway. It was summertime, so the Hay Plains road would be okay. Leaving South Hay and trundling out onto the plains, the hot summer sun beating in on him, with no breeze, and with the dust sometimes clouding around him, he noticed irrigation channels out to the right, with fast-flowing water. The main channel ran parallel with the road and was very wide and inviting.

The Hay Plains.

It crossed his mind how cooling it would be to stop and splash some water over himself. *Nice thought, but on with the job.*

An hour or so later, still driving beside the water channel, he saw some Aboriginal kids splashing around in it. He thought he might try that later up the road, and it didn't take long for the thought to become action. With the heat and the dust getting to him, he abruptly pulled over onto the grass next to the road, whipped off his shirt and shorts and jumped into the water channel in his jocks.

Now, what he hadn't realised was that the channel, as well as being wide, was deep and flowed very quickly. When he bobbed to the surface, in the instant before he was tumbled over and under again, he was already skimming along, and he could see that the truck was fast disappearing into the distance behind him. The next time he managed to come up for air the truck had completely disappeared from view.

Up and down, over and over, gasping air when he could: so he went, about as swiftly as he had been going all day in the truck. He hit the bottom in parts and bounced off again, time after time. At one point he realised he had lost his jocks, but gasping for air was more important than worrying about that.

Finally, after quite some time, he managed to grab for the clay bank, desperately clawing at it, and with his legs swept around he clung to it like a leech, then heaved himself out of the water and, on all fours, scrambled up the side. So there he was, sitting on the grass, clasping his knees to his chest, water and wet clay dripping down all over his crown jewels, wondering how he got into such a situation and where the bloody hell the truck was. It was nowhere to be seen: the dirt road stretched back empty into the heat haze.

With a sigh he stood up, and without a backward glance at the water channel he set off, trudging back up the road in the direction of the truck that he had abandoned so quickly to have a cool dip. He looked like one of those terracotta warriors lost in a foreign land.

Colin Emery

27

Homer Simpson country

In the year 2000 I was staying in Soulard, the French quarter in the charming city of St Louis, on the Mississippi. When I had arrived in the city I had taken a taxi to the hostel address and was a bit bewildered when I was dropped in a tree-lined street before a row of terraced houses all looking the same and whose numbers were a little hard to work out. I knocked on the nearest front door and waited, then knocked again. There was no answer. Puzzled, I rechecked my directions and concluded that this was the correct address. I then noticed a tiny alleyway next to the door where I was standing, so I made my way down this rough cobblestone path and ended up at a door that was probably the original back door of the house. It turned out that this was the office for the hostel, which consisted of two or three of the terraced houses. I believe the management was looking to buy more as time went on. The hostel was clean and neat, with a separate building for the kitchen and lounge area, which also had quite a large library of books.

One day, after wandering a few blocks from my hostel to a market that has operated on the same site since the area was first used by French fur trappers coming downriver from Canada in the early eighteenth century, I purchased a small silver-plated dish as a memento of my visit. Then I caught a bus into town to have a look around. Walking down to the park on the river I saw the tall Gateway Arch, a high metal memorial dedicated to the early pioneers on their way west. After squeezing into a seat inside the arch I was lifted up at an angle to the top, where there is an observation lounge. Looking through the window you can see the vast western horizon, which was the gateway to the old Wild West, where the wagon trains set out for California and Oregon.

Unsure what to do when I came down, I hailed a taxi and asked what was going on that day in town. As I glanced across the roof of the cab I could see a brightly painted paddle-steamer moored against the opposite bank of the Mississippi and wondered if it was one that travelled up and down the river. The cabbie informed me that it was a casino and permanently moored there. Because it happened to be Father's Day, all fathers were invited for a free buffet luncheon.

'That'll do me,' I said, as I climbed in. We had to drive a few blocks north and then over a bridge to the other side of the river, into East St Louis, which took us into another state—Illinois. The suburb surrounding the casino was very rundown and seemed a poor section, with boarded-up shops.

On arriving in the dining room I was greeted with a smile and asked to wait just a little time for a table. As I sat in the waiting area a black American family entered. There were grandchildren, mums and dads, and, regally bringing up the rear with a bit of a swagger, was grandfather. They were all dressed in the best of clothes, the little ones neat and tidy and the grown-ups in the latest fashions. But it was the grand-father who held my attention. He was obviously proud of his brood and, indeed, of himself. He wore a black suit with vest, showing a very large and heavy gold chain across the front, as well as many gold rings on his fingers, and a huge gold watch on his wrist surrounded by a number of gold chains. His black hat had a wide band of very bright yellow that matched his wide tie with gold tiepin. He looked as if he had stepped out of a movie from forty years earlier. No doubt he was a successful man enjoying his family outing. They were quite a joy to see.

I had a good meal there, all the more so since it was on the house, and I gave the cost of the meal to the slot machines.

•

Back at the hostel the next morning I noticed in the backyard a black, dusty Pontiac Trans Am dating from about 1986. When I asked about it I was told a backpacker from Sweden

225

had left it there a couple of years earlier and hadn't come back. The manager said if I was interested I could have it for $1000, and he would get it registered. I thought about it: I was going to be making my way to Chicago and New York and didn't think a car was such a good idea in those busy cities. It would be too hard and expensive to find parking space. So I dropped the idea.

●

Next day I decided to catch the Amtrak to Chicago. After a long walk down a deserted road and through a goods yard I came to a little building situated on a rail line with absolutely nothing around it but rail tracks, like a goods siding. It certainly wasn't prominent, like our railway stations in Australia, and gave the impression that rail wasn't that popular as a form of transport. Perhaps buses were more convenient here. In Chicago, New York and Washington, DC, the railway stations were similar to Australia's: big and busy. But for some reason as I had walked down the deserted road towards the station in St Louis I had felt a little uncomfortable, a bit uneasy, and I didn't know why.

I soon found out. I pushed the door of the building open and entered a small ticket office and waiting room, where there were three or four rows of plastic chairs, enough for twenty people or so. In the far corner of the room was the ticket counter, protected by a heavy wire-mesh grill, with a man seated behind it. The only other occupant of the room was a youngish lady reading a book.

As I put my suitcase down beside the wall just inside the door, the swing doors on the opposite side of the room, which led to the platform, burst open, and an elderly man pushed through with a young and much larger man holding on to his elbow. Both men were making straight for the ticket seller. The old man seemed distressed. I slowly lowered myself into the nearest seat to wait till they had finished at the counter. With the room being nearly empty there was no need to form a queue, as the next train wasn't due for at least a couple of hours.

I took a book out of my case. I could hear the old man complaining about something to the ticket clerk. Then he abruptly turned and made for the doors out to the platform again, still with the large young man holding firmly on to his arm, like a policeman escorting a prisoner into court. The ticket clerk hadn't said a word: just kept his head down, doing whatever he was doing.

I was about to get up and go over to the ticket window when the door I had come through opened and a tall, well-dressed man entered. As he put his case down and made for the ticket counter the platform doors burst open again, and in came the old man with the young man still hanging on to him. The old man was complaining that the young man was trying to take his ticket away from him. I wasn't sure what it was all about.

The reading lady had not lifted her eyes from her book since I had entered the room. As the well-dressed man made for the counter, the young man let go of the old man's arm and walked straight up to this new arrival, demanding in a loud voice his name and address.

The old man quickly scuttled back out to the platform. For the first time I took a closer look at this young man with the loud mouth, and I immediately sensed trouble. He was about twenty-five years old, quite tall and heavily built. He wore a brown baseball cap, and a fawn jacket and trousers. His face was puffy and pale. His eyes darted here and there all the time, squinting. His body language suggested to me that he was an idiot and a bully boy. He certainly didn't appear to be someone of authority. I overheard him say to the other man that he knew who he was and that he was being watched and had better be careful. He asked him where he was going and how much money he had in his pockets.

Now I knew for sure we had a nut case in the room. But how dangerous was he? The other man was careful to keep everything low-key and didn't get angry. He just tried to palm him off by saying he was going to Chicago for the weekend and that he was studying at the university here in St Louis.

Then the young man changed his tune. He jammed his right hand into his jacket pocket, as if going for a gun, and said loudly, 'I'm with the FBI. We have been watching you for a long time.'

While this was going on I made my way to the ticket counter and told the official that there appeared to be a problem out here with this young man and asked if he could do something about it. The clerk looked up from his desk at me and then lowered his eyes, without saying a word, as if

I wasn't there. He completely ignored me. *Hm, okay*, I thought to myself. I took a deep breath, knowing there was no help coming from the railway staff, and that there could be problems for all of us in the room. The young man was obviously tripping on some substance or had a mental problem. I looked back over my shoulder and saw that he still had his hand in his pocket. His voice was getting louder and more belligerent. The other man was trying to pick up his bag and turn for the door. I began to wonder if there really was a gun in the jacket pocket and if maybe I had better get out of there as well.

I hurried over and picked up my case, and followed them both out of the entry door. As we came out into the car park area, the young man swung around and said, 'I'm going to put you both under arrest. I'm with the FBI.' His hand was still in his jacket pocket. Aware of the loose gun laws in the USA, I was starting to get concerned that he really might be armed.

The other man and I looked at each other and had an instant understanding. I gave a quick wink to him that the young man couldn't see, meaning, 'Humour this idiot and get help.' The man made a quick call on his mobile phone behind the young man's back, while he was busy giving me a hard time about how he had been watching both of us for weeks.

I was coming to the conclusion that this could only end in some 'rough stuff'. Now, at seventy-odd years of age, rough stuff for me was long past, but if he was going to have a 'three-course meal', I was going to have a try for a 'sandwich', at least. I decided what to do, or at least what to attempt to do. I put my spectacles in my trouser pocket, then, when the time came, I would give him an embrace around the neck, two fingers in his eyes and then, as quickly as possible, a thumb in the larynx, just above the breast bone. If I was successful, that would give us time to vacate the place. I did have to accept the fact, though, that without my goggles it was quite possible that I would poke two fingers up his nose and put a thumb in his mouth. *Oh well, see what happens*, I thought. *If nothing else, he might choke.*

Then, out of the blue, our salvation arrived. A taxi appeared, the driver's door popped open and the driver looked over the roof and asked who had phoned for a cab. The well-dressed man waved at him, grabbed his bag and nodded his head for me to follow. We walked quickly to the cab as the driver opened the boot. As we put our cases in my companion said to the cabby to take us to the bus station. We made for the back doors.

As this was happening the young man just stood there, looking at us and the cab. He couldn't make up his mind what to do or who to grab. Suddenly, he went for the other man. The driver, not following what was going on, had hopped in and started the motor. I yelled loudly and angrily across the roof of the cab, 'Piss off, mate! You're a pain in the arse!' while putting my specs back on.

The young man stopped momentarily, looking at me with surprise and then anger, not sure what to do. With a rush the other man brushed past him, yanked his door open, jumped in and locked it.

The young man started to run around the back of the cab

to grab me, and I yelled, 'Quick! Out of here, driver—this guy's a nut case!' I jumped in and locked my door.

With a screech of tyres we took off. Looking back out of the rear window, we could see the young man leaning forwards, looking at us with a completely blank expression on his face. I was wondering if he was going to pull a gun out of his pocket, but he simply stood there, fumbling his right hand in his jacket pocket as if it was stuck. Then we turned a corner and lost sight of him. The cabbie said, 'There are plenty of nut cases around this area. You were lucky I was nearby.' He said he would report it to the police after dropping us off at the bus depot.

I gazed out of the window at the streets flashing past, going through my poke and jab routine, wondering was I still up to it. I'll never know if there was a gun in that pocket, but I don't think there was.

That afternoon I left St Louis in a bus bound for Chicago. A short time later we stopped for a coffee break in a small town in Illinois. Would you believe the name of the town was Springfield? That certainly suited what had been going on earlier that day. I felt like I had just featured in one of the crazy episodes of *The Simpsons*. As we travelled through the town I studied the faces of people on the footpath, certain that I would see, if not the whole Simpson family, Homer at least. I must have missed him.

28

Yatala Prison

Jim Boler was a close friend of Terry Gordon; they grew up together in Rockdale, a suburb of Sydney. After Terry started with Bruce Transport he helped Jim get a driving job with the same firm. They got into some problems occasionally, as mates do, like the time in the summer of 1956, when they took a load of agricultural pipes to Peterborough in South Australia, then loaded salt from the little town of Price to be delivered back to Sydney.

Jim was driving a green Albion HD model, and Terry was driving a white AEC Monarch. (When the Monarch was first released it was called a Mercury, but the Ford Motor Company objected, so it ended up being renamed the Monarch.) Driving back up the Yorke Peninsula, around the top end of the Gulf

St Vincent, it was easy driving: all rough, flat country with a few low-lying hills, and sparsely populated. After a couple of hours chugging along at 39 miles per hour with nothing to see but the horizon, Terry pulled over to the side of the road and Jim pulled in behind him. After a slight delay Terry climbed down from his truck and walked back to Jim's truck, carrying a folded Shell road map he had been studying while driving along. Those maps were given out freely to all travellers by the service stations back then. Terry loved to look at maps and try different roads, as there were no superhighways in those days and sometimes there were ways to shorten distances by cutting through off the beaten track. It sometimes worked, but with Terry it was always a gamble. Terry looked up at Jim and said they could maybe cut off a lot of useless miles by turning left a bit further on. It was mostly a dirt road but should be okay.

Jim was quite happy to accept Terry's suggestion. He was anxious to get home and have a couple of days off. 'Okay, I'll follow you,' he said, gazing out across the plain. 'What's that, way over there?' he asked, pointing to a large cluster of buildings, the only ones that could be seen, whichever way he looked.

'That's Yatala Prison complex,' replied Terry. 'Tough place, I hear.'

They set off again. After about thirty minutes Terry slowed down and turned left onto a sealed road that seemed to head straight for the horizon, roughly in the direction they wanted to go. It was a bit narrow, definitely a secondary road, but never mind—it was going eastwards, and that's the way they were headed.

After another hour the road narrowed to a gravel track, but still not a bad surface. The wind was blowing the wrong way for Jim, as he seemed to be in a constant cloud of dust thrown up by Terry's wheels.

Then the road started to get narrow again, till finally it was just a single-lane dirt track, and the most they could manage was second gear. By this time Jim was getting a little anxious. The track seemed always to be wandering around a little to the right. They had been bouncing along for what seemed like hours, and things were not getting any better. He tried to get Terry's attention—flicking the headlights on, blowing the horn—but to no avail. Terry just kept plodding along.

After a while, with relief Jim noticed that the track had improved to a narrow dirt road again, but he was still enveloped in Terry's dust. Then, a little further on, it improved once more, upgrading to a wider gravel road, though still dusty and rough. *Okay, not so bad. Maybe the worst part is over*, thought Jim, seeing a sealed T-intersection coming up. Terry was slowing down, so Jim came to a stop and lit a cigarette, relaxed a little, and wiped his face with a towel.

Terry jumped down and walked back towards Jim's truck. 'Um, must be something wrong somewhere,' said Terry with a weak-looking grin.

'Why, what's up?' said Jim, glancing down at his mate.

'Well, if you look down the road there, to the right a couple of hundred yards, you can see a road going off parallel to this one and going the way we just came.'

'So?'

'That's the road we took about four hours ago,' said Terry, with a bit of an embarrassed giggle.

Jim looked slightly further to his right, and, sure enough, in the distance was the Yatala Prison complex. It was at a slightly different angle from the first time they'd spotted it, but it was definitely Yatala Prison, and still the only thing to be seen on the whole horizon.

Jim cleared his throat, looked down at Terry, shook his head, put the Albion into gear and took off, leaving Terry standing in the middle of the road. Jim's truck brushed past the Monarch, turned left onto the original sealed road they had left four hours earlier, and with quick puffs of exhaust as he changed up the gears, telling Terry he wasn't very popular at the moment, Jim went on his way.

Terry caught up later in the day—much later: it was nearly nightfall.

•

But this trip wasn't over yet; it was over 1000 miles to Sydney, and Terry carried on map-reading when he had the chance, which Jim was no longer exactly happy about. Time and miles crawled by. The salt was a heavy load, and across the flatlands of South Australia and the state of Victoria it was slow going. Both trucks were loaded to the limit and probably more. It was a little difficult to estimate the weight exactly, as the bags of salt were filled by hand. The nearest weighbridge was hundreds of miles away, in Port Augusta. The general idea in those days was to hand-load and hope for the best. The bosses preferred a

Jim's Albion HD (left) and Terry's AEC Monarch. You can see the rough, flat land and part of the secondary gravel road in the background. The side mirrors on the Monarch were state-of-the-art back then. There's a high tank aerial on the Albion for the primitive radio reception. When all the aerial's sections were joined together, it was 20 feet off the ground, but even then the reception wasn't the best. The aerials could be purchased from ex-army surplus stores.

truck to be loaded to the limit so the maximum money could be earnt from each trip. It was the driver's responsibility to dodge the police and transport inspectors any way he could and get the load through.

Jim and Terry pressed on, eventually arriving at Buronga, a small community across the Murray River, the border between the Victorian town of Mildura and the state of

New South Wales. No police or transport inspectors had been seen: so far so good. They now faced the Hay Plains, a long and lonely stretch of gravel road that would take them further east to join up with the busy Hume Highway, the last section, which would take them north to Sydney, home, and a couple of days off.

But nature got in the way. It had been raining for days, and the Hay Plains were notorious for being impassable in the wet. Light rain could turn the road into a quagmire of black mud. This time, the plains were completely flooded. It would take at least a week after the rain stopped to even think about trying to cross it.

So the map came out again. Terry was in his element. 'Okay,' he said, after much finger movement around the map, 'instead of east then north to Sydney, it looks like we have to go south.'

'You've got to be joking,' said Jim. 'Why south?'

'Well, there's no roads north that will get us around it. But if we duck down over the border again and zigzag east, we'll come out somewhere on the north highway.'

'Hm. No more Yatala Prison roads, okay?'

Taking a southbound route they travelled along roads that had never seen trucks that size, thundering through tiny hamlets and towns that the boys hadn't heard of before. Hour after hour, they plodded on.

The trailers used eight-stud wheels, and back then the studs had a tendency to break, and then the wheel would split around the holes. That happened to Terry just out of the town of Deniliquin, but luckily a blacksmith welded it together again.

They had decided to make for the town of Wagga Wagga. If they could get there they would be back on sealed roads. The trouble was that they were travelling north again, and back into waterlogged country. They were just hoping they had skirted around the worst part. They eventually made it to Lockhart, only about 60 miles west of Wagga, but were told the road was covered in water all the way; it was impassable. The rain had nearly stopped, so they decided to give it a go and took off slowly, splashing along; at times, the only way to judge where the road went was by the tops of white road posts poking out above the water. It was touch and go in places, with the water level just below the trailer loads of salt.

It was close to midnight when they saw a light up ahead. As they approached it they could see that a large barricade had been set up across the road, and a police car was parked next to it. 'Where the hell did you two come from?' demanded the highway patrol officer as they pulled to a halt.

'Lockhart,' said Terry. 'Why?'

'That road you've just come along has been closed for days. You can't get through.'

'Um, well, we did,' replied Terry with a grin, and with that the boys idled off, breathing a sigh of relief and that feeling of *Ain't we smart?*

29

Before Underbelly

I was in Melbourne loading new Standard Vanguard sedans for Sydney. It was about 3 pm on a Thursday in 1951. The Commer R7 had a slant six cylinder petrol motor under the seat and was quite comfortable for sleeping, with the seat just long enough if you kept your legs bent. I had been lying down waiting for more cars. Two sedans had been run onto the bottom deck, but then there was a wait for the three for the top deck. It seemed there was a problem on the production line.

Finally, the loader came out and told me I would have to come back in the morning for the other cars. I trundled back to the office in Bridge Road, Richmond, to bring them up to date on the loading problems. It was decided

I had better book in to a hotel for the night. The hotel across the road couldn't help; they were full with a crowd visiting for the weekend football game. The office tried a few other hotels close by but no luck—must have been a big game that weekend. It was then that Rupert the accountant said he knew where I might get a bed. He gave me an address, telling me that it was a kind of B & B that a respectable elderly lady ran for visiting PMG employees from the bush who came to Melbourne for their exams. So off I went in the truck to find this B & B.

It was on a boulevard type of a street—very wide with a large garden and trees down the centre. In fact, it was so wide that vehicles were allowed to park next to the centre garden as well as on the footpath side, and there was still plenty of room for traffic. I found the address and parked next to the centre garden opposite the house.

The grey-haired lady who ran the B & B was a darling. As she explained, two men had been delayed coming to the city for their exams so she had a couple of beds to spare that night. We had a great dinner in the big kitchen, with the table seating about ten of us, all talking and asking questions of each other. They were quite amazed at my truck and the job I did delivering cars all the way to Sydney. None of them had ever been out of their country town before.

After dinner I went out and sat on the front step, looking over the road at my truck, stuck there with these two brand-new cars on the bottom deck. They didn't look very safe to me. I was worried someone could if not steal a car then somehow rip the wheels off for the tyres. Everything was hard to buy at that time, and tyres were very sought after.

One of the other men from the B & B came out and sat down next to me. 'What's up?'

'I'm worried about the cars; I can see someone stealing something off them. I think I'd better sleep in the truck tonight, just to be on the safe side.'

After a little while he went back inside to talk to the men still sitting around the kitchen table.

Then the lady of the house came out to where I was. 'One of the boys tells me you think you might sleep in the truck tonight. You're worried that the cars may be damaged.'

'Yes, I'm not too happy. It's a big responsibility till I get them delivered in Sydney.'

'Now, you look here, young man: you come in and have a good night's sleep. Nothing is going to happen to your truck or the cars. This whole street is protecting them. No one, and I mean no one, would dare touch any vehicle of someone who is staying with me. Now come on in. Everything is okay.'

She sounded so sure that I put my fears away and went in and slept well, finishing off loading the next morning. On returning to the office for my paperwork I thanked Rupert and said it had been great. Then I laughed and told him of my intention to sleep in the truck till the old lady had talked me into getting to bed.

Rupert smiled and said, 'I'll let you in on a secret. Your truck, the cars and you were in the safest place in Melbourne. As you were told, everyone in the street was watching over you.

You could have left the truck unlocked and the doors open, even the new cars. Nothing would have been touched.'

'Oh yeah? How come?' I asked, unconvinced.

'Well, the lady—now, she is a lovely and highly respectable person, but her two sons are notorious. They are the toughest and most dangerous criminals in Melbourne, and nobody would be game to cross them or upset their mother. You and your truck were as safe as if you'd been in Buckingham Palace.'

No wonder everything had been safe out there on my boulevard of dreams.

30

Border crossing

During the 1950s my parents decided to move from Sydney to tropical Queensland. Dad and I decided the best idea was to buy a truck in Sydney, load everything on, drive it to the new house, unload it, and then sell the truck up there. We found a 5-ton International K–5 flat-top, ex-army, with low miles and in good condition. It was still painted that flat, dirty-brown colour, khaki, but it would do for what we needed. The price was right, so Dad purchased it. He found it amusing that he was now in the trucking game, sort of.

You should have seen us when we set out for Queensland: we looked like we were out of that movie with Henry Fonda, *The Grapes of Wrath*, about farmers back in the 1930s who had to leave their farms in Oklahoma for California, looking for a better life after their land turned into a dust bowl. They had Grandad sitting in a chair on top of the load on a rickety old truck. We were nearly the same: we had the old outdoor setting, which we nearly forgot, roped on top of the tarpaulin covering the furniture, but no grandad on top. Mum went by car later on. It was just Dad—who had an artificial leg—and me in the cabin of the old K-5. (Dad had lost his left leg to cancer years before. He never did like his spare leg and preferred crutches.)

At this time any truck carrying goods further than 50 miles by road in the state of New South Wales had to pay a tax for every extra mile of the journey. If it was going interstate the tax was calculated to the border. It had to be paid before the journey, and the journey made within stipulated dates. The permit had to be carried with the vehicle and would be checked numerous times on the journey by the transport inspectors who patrolled the highways. Even Dad, according to the law, had to apply for a permit to move his own goods more than 50 miles, although the tax for that was not a large amount compared to general goods carted for profit. However, I didn't tell Dad this, as I wanted him to be innocent of any wrongdoing. But I had in mind a chance to get back at the inspectors who had been giving me hell for years. They treated us like renegades or outlaws, and we reacted by giving as good as we got.

Anyway, Dad hopped aboard with his crutches, and we set off on a bright spring morning for the great trek to tropical Queensland, over 600 miles away. State border, here we come!

•

It was late afternoon as we approached the little town of Karuah. I knew that inspectors usually waited near the town, on top of a hill that had a gravel area to pull off and where they could also weigh trucks with portable scales if they thought they were overweight. Sure enough, they were there: two inspectors in a dark-coloured four-door, and as we climbed towards the top I saw one get out of the car with his grey dustcoat on, ready to wave me in to the gravelled area, a metal 'stop' sign in his hand. As we approached, the sign was dramatically hoisted into the air and a dustcoated arm waved us in to the parking area.

I quickly explained to Dad about the inspectors, and of course he remembered all the stories I had told him of the hard times they had given me. 'Ignore them,' he said. 'This is my truck and my goods, and I will not let them interfere with my lawful business.'

I looked sideways at Dad, who had a smile on his face. I gave him a wink, a grin and a nod. Then I asked, 'You sure?'

'Why not, son, after all the strife they have heaped on you boys over the years? Let's do it.'

So we both looked straight ahead, ignoring the figure on the side of the road. I changed up a gear and took off down the other side of the hill. I couldn't see along the passenger side of the truck, as there was no mirror, but looking into my side mirror all of sudden I saw a cloud of dust in the air as the black four-door bounced onto the road with the obvious intent of catching us. *Now*, I thought, *what's coming is going to be the best part. I have wanted to do this for years.* They were overtaking me, but with my hands on the wheel at ten past ten, as all new drivers are taught, I carried on, looking straight ahead, innocent like.

I heard a voice yelling out, 'Pull over, driver!'

I kept looking straight ahead, as if I hadn't heard a thing. The car eased off and tucked in behind us; they were thinking I was about to pull over. But this black duck just kept going.

Next thing, they were up beside us again. 'Pull over, driver! I am a transport inspector.'

This time I looked towards the voice with a blank expression on my face, like the one my dad used to say I wore when I had done wrong as a kid. I just looked and then turned back to concentrate on my driving, something a driver would do if he was new at driving a big truck.

The car accelerated and pulled in front of us, slowing down slightly, with the 'stop' sign on the end of a grey arm waving vigorously above the roof of the car. The arm appeared to be quite agitated. I smiled at Dad, who was also smiling, then I quickly moved out and overtook this strange car with these strange people in it who seemed to be playing silly games.

Up they came again, the front passenger in his dustcoat waving his sign and yelling, 'STOP!'

This time, with all the pent-up fury and frustration of years of torment from running fourteen- and eighteen-wheelers all over the country and being hounded by them day and night,

I glanced down at this figure waving his sign and very clearly, very loudly and very angrily yelled back at the top of my voice, 'GET STUFFED! Get out of my way!' (That felt so good.) Then, like any careful driver, I turned my full attention to the road ahead, concentrating on my driving. But not before I saw his mouth drop open in shock and disbelief.

I turned to Dad and said, 'Okay, I'll pull up on the road here just ahead to make it awkward for them.' (There was very little traffic on the roads back then, so there was no danger to anybody; it was just them and us out there on an otherwise deserted road.) I stopped the truck, left the motor running, climbed down onto the road and walked back to where they had halted behind us, half on and half off the road. I was wearing scruffy old pants and shirt, and Dad was in something similar. 'Who the hell are you, yelling at me to pull over? You think you're the police or something? I've got a good mind to call in to the next police station and report you for dangerous driving!' Those were my first angry words to the two inspectors, who were now walking towards me.

'We are transport inspectors,' was the reply, as they homed in on a couple of suspected road tax dodgers. (They were right about that, but we were not going to admit it.)

'I don't give a damn! You're a menace on the roads. How dare you yell at me to stop? Who are you and what do you want? And make it quick,' I replied, loudly. I was wondering, while this was going on, how long I could string it out. But I was determined to give it my best shot.

'We have to sight your permit.'

'What bloody permit? Are you nuts or something? Anybody can see we are not carrying livestock, if that's what you think. You're not much good as an inspector if you can't tell the difference between private people going about their business and livestock carriers.'

'We are not livestock inspectors.'

'Well, who the bloody hell are you and what the bloody hell do you want?'

'Where did you start your journey?'

'Sydney. Why? What's it to you?' (We were well over 100 miles from where we'd started.)

'Where is your permit, then, to carry goods by road on a journey over 50 miles?'

'What?'

'Your permit.'

'No idea what you're talking about. Permit? What the hell is a permit?'

'What load are you carrying?'

'Furniture.'

'You have to have a permit to carry furniture.'

'Garbage. Who says?'

'The law says.'

'Rubbish. Do you mean to tell me that because Dad and I are moving to Queensland we have to pay this bloody awful state money just to get out of it? You're dreaming!'

Just then Dad came around the front of the truck and down the road to where we were standing, swinging quickly and expertly on his crutches, with an angry look on his face.

I was proud of him. 'What's going on, son? Who are these men? What do they want?' He was playing it to the hilt.

'We are transport inspectors,' one of the men called out loudly.

'So go and inspect some transport somewhere. My son and I have a long way to go and we haven't got time to waste on you people.' My dad was from the old school; he could rip you to bits with the English language and you wouldn't know what hit you.

'Well, sir,' the inspector said, in a gentler tone, 'a permit is needed to carry goods more than 50 miles on any one journey.'

'Well, that's fine,' said Dad. 'Good to hear it. We are not carrying goods; we are carrying *my* furniture on *my* truck to Queensland, where I will spend my retirement years. Now, Ray, come on, we have a long way to go, and you young men are wasting our valuable time.'

With that, Dad spun around on his crutches, and we both headed back to the cabin of the old K-5. I didn't dare look around. When I was behind the wheel I glanced into the small rear-view mirror out of the corner of my eye, not moving my head, and the two inspectors were still standing where we'd left them. There was an earnest discussion going on, with many a glance towards the cabin. I engaged low gear and took off slowly, leaving the two dustcoated figures in the middle of the road not knowing what to do.

'How did we do?' asked my dad after a few miles, with a smile all over his face.

'Great, mate,' I replied, laughing. 'Fantastic. You should have been a truck driver.'

The inspectors eventually followed us into Karuah, and I was sure they would get the police, but no, they pulled in to the pub. They probably needed a drink after their run-in with us.

•

There was one more road block to pass. Inspectors always waited on top of Ballina hill, and the next afternoon, sure enough, they stopped us. One was in the middle of the road with a 'stop' sign, pointing to the parking area. I didn't pull off the road, just sort of ambled up to him, leant out of the window and, before the inspector could speak, looked down and said, 'Are you another one of the Gestapo, running around checking what everyone is doing in this state? We had a run-in yesterday with some of your lot down near Karuah; they were happy to see the back of us. This is my dad's truck with his furniture, and he is migrating to Queensland, out of this bloody awful state. I suggest you just stand aside. The border is three hours away, and we intend to cross over tonight come what may.' With that I slipped it into gear and moved off, leaving him in the middle of the road with a surprised look on his face, the 'stop' sign dangling beside his leg. We watched the road behind for a time, but no one chased us.

We crossed the border into Queensland a little after 8 pm that night—all smiles.

•

My dad enjoyed his retirement. He sold the truck for a small profit, and over the years we had a few laughs thinking about that trip and coming up with things we could have said but then agreeing that, no, it had been good enough. When I'm drinking a beer and happen to think of that trip, the beer always tastes so much better.

31

The edge of darkness

Johnny McCullock and I were making for Brisbane when we heard that the transport inspectors were waiting for us up ahead. I was a wanted man, and Johnny was overloaded. We decided that if we took the little ferry at Karuah and detoured a little we would outflank them. We did, too, but we nearly sank the ferry. The ferryman nearly had a fainting fit when he saw us emerge out of the midnight darkness. There was nowhere for us to turn around, so he had to get us across somehow. A bit of folding money and a slug of scotch and leaving the ferry's gates open did the trick.

Once we were across it took all night to crawl along the rough track that wended its way north. Around 3 am Johnny's Mercedes-Benz 315 ran out of puff up a steep climb, so he backed it down a little and I squeezed past to hook on to him, and with a lot of sweating, cursing and hoping we staggered to the top. It was easier going after that, and we eventually poked our noses out onto the highway again about 100 miles north of where we had disappeared into the unknown. The good news was that we had outsmarted the enemy. They were still back there waiting for us, and we were on our way north, hidden by the friendly night. That was one to us.

•

The night-time wasn't always so friendly to us truck drivers, though, especially out in the desert. The truck cabins were divided in half by a large metal motor cover that made sleeping a problem, because it was impossible to make a flat bed, and trips could take weeks or even months if a truck broke down. At first, when I drove across the desert, I slept under the trailer with a couple of blankets, till I realised that snakes and scorpions and other unknowns roamed out there at night. My wake-up call came when a scorpion wriggled past my face in the dark one night, scaring the hell out of me. If you were bitten by one of them you'd be dead before anyone found you.

After that I slept on a flat surface on top of the loaded trailer, away from anything that might want a bit of me. To start with I was worried that I might roll off the top of the load in my sleep and break my neck, but I fixed that problem by tying a loose rope over the load and tucking myself in my sleeping bag under it, with my Colt .45 pistol under the pillow.

Then there are the problems created by an active mind that has been alone for too long. It can conjure up vivid pictures sometimes. A mate of mine got scared one night. He hadn't seen anyone for days. He ran off into the scrub, thinking that some creature had touched him on the shoulder from behind as he finished wiping the headlights. It took him an hour to pluck up the courage to circle the truck, stumbling over bushes in the darkness, and then run for the cabin, absolutely terrified something was out there waiting to grab him. He kept driving till dawn's light before he relaxed. He realised the next day it had been the metal hand signal on the driver's door that had touched his shoulder when the door moved just a fraction of an inch.

At night I had seen, mixed with the bright stars, ghostly lights that seemingly moved, like spaceships, over near the horizon—moving, then hovering, then moving again. I could never work out what they were. They sent shivers up my spine, and I would close my eyes tight and bury my head into the pillow, not wanting to look at something I didn't understand and hoping that the next time I opened my eyes it would be a new day.

Sometimes of a night I'd be standing beside the cabin of the truck, rugged up in flying boots, thick pants and leather jacket, with a freezing-cold wind blowing in from the Antarctic ice, when, without warning, the wind would stop. The air would suddenly become completely still, like a tropical night, hot and motionless, so hot that my jacket, pants and fur-lined boots instantly became uncomfortable to wear. Then the air would stir again, but now much softer, a gentle, warm, caressing breeze. That's when I'd quickly look around into the blackness beyond the headlights, towards the moving lights, then up above into the dark heavens, dreading what might be hovering up there. A quick scramble for the cabin, slam the door and lock it, to keep out the unknown that I could feel was out there but couldn't see or understand. Heart pumping faster, adrenalin racing through the veins, at what? I didn't know. It was just spooky. None of it made sense. Cold wind, hot wind, no wind; lights moving, bushes rustling. *Let's get out of here* was the next thought. *Anything could be out there.*

I stopped out in the middle of nowhere one night, turned the motor off, switched all the lights off, and wandered up the road, admiring the stars—not a care in the world. But then I lost sight of the truck in the extreme black of the night and was completely disorientated, not knowing which way to go to get back. Panic is a terrible thing. I wanted to run to my comfort zone, my truck, but which way was it? I managed to control my panic and my fear of snakes, and felt along the edge of the track with my boots, stumbling here and there, till I finally made it back to her, my darling, the truck I had named the Moonlight Gambler. She had been only a few feet away. I never made that mistake again: always left the lights on and the motor running if I stopped at night for any reason. I also tried never to get out of the cabin at night if possible.

On a very still night—not a breath of wind—while checking the load I saw a large shrub about 20 feet away in the gloomy darkness. It was shaking violently, the only shrub showing any movement among the many others nearby. I blasted it with my pistol, pumped the whole magazine into it, quite positive there was something large and primitive out there ready to do me harm. After the last shot I bolted for the cabin of the truck, jumped in, slammed the door and drove till dawn.

The Moonlight Gambler, Albion HD 53 model, with the last load of whale oil, 1957. The cabin had one of the first homemade sleeper bunk cabins in Australia. The rear of the cabin was cut out and extended, and two 44-gallon drums were fitted beneath the extension. One held extra fuel, and the other was fitted with a tap and carried water. That, along with a primus stove, tinned food, coffee, tea, sugar, powdered milk and one or two guns, made me completely self-sufficient.

•

A little over halfway across the Nullarbor Plain was a straight section of track that was 90 miles long. It seemed to go on forever. On one trip out there, on a hot afternoon in the summer of 1957, near the western end of that 90-mile straight, I saw a moving brown cloud. Maybe it was an updraft of air stirring up the dust—we called them willy-willies—or maybe it was a traveller coming my way. I hadn't seen anybody for days. I concentrated on the dust cloud to see if it moved right or left off the track, but it was coming directly towards me. Could it be a vehicle? I hoped it was. I willed it to be—and it was! Yippee! Somebody to talk to. It was wonderful out there to actually see and talk to someone and feel you were not alone in the world. Anyone you met was greeted as a long-lost friend. It's hard to explain the loneliness.

I was travelling east, driving an Albion HD model with a five-speed gearbox and worm drive differential, pulling a tandem 32-foot trailer loaded with 44-gallon drums of whale oil. This was the last consignment of whale oil from Western Australia to the eastern states: Australia was ceasing whale hunting as an industry. One drum leaked a little into the floorboards on that trip, and over the years that followed every time it rained there was a very fishy smell. Joe, the driver of the other truck, was travelling west in a similar model to mine, with a 32-foot trailer carrying a high load of crated refrigerators.

It was early afternoon, very hot—a good time to have a

talk, especially as meeting someone was such a rare event. We boiled the billy and made a cup of tea. Joe was short, with red hair and freckles, a bit on the plump side, if you know what I mean. It was his first trip into the unknown. He looked very worn and tired, with bloodshot eyes. I didn't think much about it, as we all seemed to take on that appearance out there. The days passed slowly and there were constant troubles to be overcome: it was probably the responsibility weighing heavily on us that made us look haggard. Plus the ever-present dust.

After sipping his hot tea, Joe looked around, took a deep breath and asked hesitantly if I had ever seen anything unusual of a night out here. Now, being an old hand, I instantly nodded my head knowingly and laughed a little, thinking of the many weird things on the plain and how night-time seemed to bring out the worst imaginings. Lying on top of a high, loaded trailer at night, gazing around, you felt like you were suspended in the black night.

Joe had stopped the previous night to check his load. He turned the motor off but left the headlights on. It was one of those still, cold nights; not a sound could be heard. He walked down the side of the trailer, testing the tightness of the ropes. Somehow, he tripped over a rock in the sand and sprawled into the darkness under the trailer. As he was collecting his wits, something wriggled past him in a panic, so close that his face was peppered with sand. With a terrified yell he pushed himself off the ground with a heave, and in doing so cracked his head against the metal spare-wheel carrier under the trailer. He staggered to his feet, rubbing his head and eyes, trying to see properly. A ghost of a breeze disturbed the still night air, and it seemed to get darker, if that was possible. He ran for the cabin door, fumbling for the handle. He hoisted himself up into the cabin with a rush and was sure, despite his watery eyes still being full of sand, that he saw the road ahead move abruptly sideways. *No. It couldn't*, his brain said, but then, as he landed in the driver's seat, it moved again. An earth tremor? Couldn't be. There seemed to be something darker than the night out there, a large, thick cloud hovering above the truck. He felt as if it was going to swallow him and the truck whole.

Did something large and unthinkable nudge the truck? was his next terrified thought. But what could be out there so large and powerful that it could inquisitively nudge a 30-ton truck? Looking out into the darkness with his watery eyes, blinking nonstop, he seemed to see some large *thing* or *things* moving. There were round, white spots at different heights that seemed to be reflecting his headlights. Were they eyes? They seemed to blink on and off all together, then in a sort of sequence.

It was all too much. He shoved the gear lever into low gear, pressed the starter button and took off as fast as he could change up through the gears. Could something monstrous or alien be watching his set of dusty, red tail-lights slowly disappearing into the night?

Joe had driven all night after that, now and then splashing water into his red, raw eyes from a bottle he kept on the seat, continually looking in the rear-view mirror and through the side windows, right and left, scared out of his mind.

So that was why he looked tired and had red-rimmed eyes. He was sure it was not the bump on his head or the sand in his eyes that had made him see things. In fact, he reckoned it was the atomic bombs they were letting off just over the horizon.

I hadn't given a thought to those bombs. Britain was using a vast area in the desert just a few hundred miles north of where we were for atomic experiments, including setting

Atomic bomb detonation, Maralinga, South Australia, 1957
(reported in The Central Queensland Herald.)

off seven atomic bombs. It was difficult to find an isolated area in the world of the twentieth century to conduct such experiments. The Australian government had agreed to the request to use our desert and had notified the public to keep away. They had also endeavoured to warn the few tribes of Aboriginals that roamed the area to vacate the land and not go back for a number of years. I sometimes wondered whether those wandering people had understood the warning. They were nomads; it was their way of life to be always on the move.

Anyway, according to Joe's thinking, things could be happening underground or out there that we didn't know about, or creatures could be mutating into who knew what diabolical shapes and sizes, stirring only in the blackness of night. He painted a vivid word picture of what could be happening out there in Never Never Land. His voice rose a little as the words tumbled out. 'There could be little gecko lizards growing as big as crocodiles, or scorpions tall enough to strike through the driver's window, or what about that mythical animal the Aboriginals call the bunyip? No one has ever seen it, but it's out there somewhere, maybe bigger and more terrifying than anyone can imagine. Could be, couldn't it?'

It was bloody hot that day, but I shivered listening to Joe. The death adder is a small but deadly venomous snake about 2 feet long, but my personal horror of snakes immediately conjured up pictures of a death adder as big as a boa constrictor. That was enough for me. I shuddered again and told Joe to shut up and drink up—it was time for us to go and make a mile.

I was heading into the area that Joe had just left, so

I checked my rifle and pistol before starting. We set off, each going his separate way. For as long as I could I kept Joe's dust cloud in sight in the wobbly little rear-view mirror. I bet he did the same to me. It was always sort of sad, and then that lonely feeling took over again, after meeting and talking with someone out there even for a short time. I decided to put at least 100 miles under my belt if possible before I stopped, so I would be out of Joe's scary country.

•

Many a night while crossing the desert after meeting Joe I wondered what Pandora's Box might have been opened by those atomic experiments. Was there something out there we hadn't seen yet, ready to envelop or pounce on the unwary? I never left the truck without carrying my pistol after that meeting, but I never saw any scary mutant creatures. I looked hard, though! And never again did I sleep up on top of the trailer. It was too close to the unknown and the edge of darkness. I would stop at sundown, lock the doors, pull the blanket over my head and go to sleep, pistol under the pillow, rifle close at hand, waiting for daylight.

Over the years I thought about what Joe had said that day, because I never saw Joe again—not once, in all my years on the road. Did he make it across the Nullarbor Plain? Perhaps he gave the east–west run away. Or maybe one of those *things* got hold of him, after all.